SHARING *experiences*

BILL LUCAS   BRIAN KEANEY

Nelson

Thomas Nelson and Sons Ltd
Nelson House Mayfield Road
Walton-on-Thames Surrey
KT12 5PL UK

51 York Place
Edinburgh
EH1 3JD UK

Thomas Nelson (Hong Kong) Ltd
Toppan Building 10/F
22A Westlands Road
Quarry Bay Hong Kong

Thomas Nelson Australia
102 Dodds Street
South Melbourne
Victoria 3205 Australia

Nelson Canada
1120 Birchmount Road
Scarborough Ontario
M1K 5G4 Canada

© Bill Lucas and Brian Keaney 1991

First published by Thomas Nelson and Sons Ltd 1991

ISBN 0-17-433068-5

NPN 9 8 7 6 5 4 3 2 1

All rights reserved. No paragraph of this publication may be reproduced, copied or transmitted save with written permission or in accordance with the provisions of the Copyright, Design and Patents Act 1988, or under the terms of any licence permitting limited copying issued by the Copyright Licensing Agency, 33-34 Alfred Place, London WC1E 7DP.

Any person who does any unauthorised act in relation to this publication may be liable to criminal prosecution and civil claims for damages.

Printed in Hong Kong

To the Student

Opportunities is an exciting new series of core books specially written to help you do well in your English lessons. *Sharing Experiences* is one of three books in the *Opportunities* series.

Opportunities will make sure that you are well prepared for the National Curriculum and for the Standard Assessment Tasks you will be taking when you are fourteen. It will not cover everything that you will need to learn. We assume that you will also be doing a variety of other work at school and at home. To be really good in English you need to keep coming back to things you have learned to improve them.

We want you to be fully involved in this book, so we have made sure that it is very clear to use. You can use the Contents Page (on pages vi and vii), and at the start of each Unit there is a list of what you will have the opportunity to learn and practise.

At the end of every Unit you will find a list of the skills that you have been learning. You can discuss these with a friend or with your teacher; sometimes you may need to ask for more help.

Record sheets

At the end of every third Unit there is a Record Sheet. You will be given special copies of these to fill in. These will help you understand what you are doing and how much progress you are making. They will also help you to learn new words to describe what you are doing.

Your teacher will probably ask you to complete one at least every term. Once you have got to know how it works, you may want to fill one in more often.

Each sheet has a number of statements on it. You will recognise these from the ends of each Unit. Next to each one there are three targets for you to aim for. This is what they mean:

I understand this and have practised it.

I have done this with help.

I feel able to do this again.

If you are not sure what a statement means or whether you can do what it says, discuss it with your teacher.

These Record Sheets will help you to know how you are getting on in your National Curriculum English. We suggest you should also keep examples of your best pieces of work and a record of what you have been reading.

Remember, you carry on learning English all your life. You will keep coming back to the same skills and improving them.

Finally, we hope you enjoy these books.

To the Teacher

Opportunities has been written specifically to cater for the requirements of Key Stage 3 English in the National Curriculum.

We believe that the teaching of English – an international language with an extraordinary range of literature – is one of the most exciting activities for teachers in all phases of education. We hope the course reflects the excitement we feel for the subject.

Opportunities provides the core of what is required for Key Stage 3 of the National Curriculum.

◆ It provides opportunities for students to experience the activities in the Programmes of Study for Key Stage 3 and so develop the skills essential for their success.

◆ It covers the range of knowledge, skills and understanding necessary for students to be able to tackle Levels 3 to 8 in the five Attainment Targets

AT1 Speaking and Listening

AT2 Reading

AT3 Writing

AT4/5 Handwriting/Presentation

A series of three books such as these cannot hope to cover the complete range of activities, particularly in Attainment Target 2, which you will want to provide in your English lessons.

We assume that *Opportunities* will provide the core of the work you will want to tackle with your students.

Opportunities has been written with the model of English learning implied by the Programmes of Study in the National Curriculum firmly in mind.

We believe that this is essentially a model of English as it is really used. It follows that we have selected real language activities where the learner knows the context, audience and purpose of the tasks s/he is being asked to attempt. The student is also given the opportunity for reflection within the different activities.

Allied to this we present language learning as a recursive activity. Young people, like adults, constantly learn more about how English can be spoken and written. They will therefore keep needing to come back to develop their competence in key areas. This is, of course reflected in the way that the Attainment Targets have been written.

There are three ways in which Opportunities is radically different from other English courses:

◆ It tackles knowledge about language.

◆ Students know what they are learning and can assess how they are progressing.

◆ All three Profile Components– speaking and listening, reading, writing – are presented as equally valuable and integrated naturally throughout the course. There are also more sustained pieces of language work in all books.

Opportunities is divided into three books to be used with the three years of Key Stage 3. The first book, *Sharing Experiences*, caters for Levels 3 to 5. It also covers work already covered at lower levels and provides opportunities for extension activities suitable for much higher levels.

The opportunities which this book presents are listed on the Contents page. Below are details of opportunities in Books 2 and 3.

Book 2, *Taking Shape*

◆ using speech marks

◆ studying the history of English

◆ looking at English today

◆ understanding dialect

◆ making sense of evidence

◆ exploring oral stories

◆ making a poetry anthology

◆ writing letters

◆ developing non-fiction writing

To the Teacher

- improving story writing
- Operation Airwaves – an exploration of news, current affairs and radio involving script development, looking at listening habits, teamwork, making a radio magazine programme, looking at and making news bulletins.

Book 3, *Presenting Ideas*

- work with diaries and autobiography
- making a television programme
- looking at words closely, e.g. etymology, dialect
- recognising and using similes and metaphors
- the craft of narrative in prose and poetry
- literature, both classic (e.g. studying a scene from Shakespeare, a poem by Lawrence) and contemporary/multicultural (including interview with an Asian poet)
- writers and animals – work on fable and satire
- understanding the way words change, including paraphrasing and using synonyms
- developing an argument
- registers of formality
- bias and point of view
- keeping a talking log
- Operation Brainwash – an extended simulation in which the students are asked to solve the mystery of the disappearance of a young girl. This involves problem-solving, writing reports, prioritising, writing letters and devising a television advertisement.

Each book has nine Units. In the last three Units there is always a major sustained piece of work. It is not necessary to use Units in the order they appear, although you will find that some skills, for example, drafting, are developed in more complex ways in the later Units.

Clear signposting throughout the books makes them versatile enough to be used as an entire course or by individual students as a resource. At the start of each Unit there is a list of opportunities. These correspond to the Programmes of Study for Key Stage 3, but are written in a language that is accessible to students.

At the end of each Unit we have built in a moment of reflection and discussion for you and your students. The skills which have been practised are listed, again in a simple but precise language. This time you will find that they correspond closely to the language of the Attainment Targets.

The model of drafting we have followed is the one suggested by the National Writing Project and the National Curriculum Council. It encourages writers to understand the process of writing. Different writers will write in different ways. The drafting model we have adopted should be seen as a guide, not a rigid formula.

At the end of every three Units we have included assesment materials to help students monitor their own progress. These record sheets exist as a separate pack of photocopy masters and are provided free with *Opportunities*.

The language on these sheets corresponds with the language used at the end of each Unit. We assume that individual teachers will establish their own patterns of use for these. You may wish to use them in conjunction with your own records when it comes to writing reports and completing Standard Assessment Tasks. We would suggest that students are encouraged to keep a file of their coursework/tasks.

We would also suggest that opportunities for student reflection, in addition to those which occur naturally throughout English lessons, should be provided at least once a term. In some cases it will be appropriate to use the record sheets when a Unit has been completed. Once they are familiar with them, many students will wish to update their progress more regularly.

Throughout *Opportunities* all students will find something to enjoy and succeed at.

We hope to produce confident, articulate young people with a view of the world in which women and men are valued equally and in which all cultures are respected.

Bill Lucas
Brian Keaney

Contents

Unit 1 Starting Out

Opportunities	2
Learning to Remember	2
My Memories Emily, age 11	2
Drawing a Time-line	3
Centre of Attention	4
Successful Groupwork	4
Remembering in detail	5
The Memory Game	5
Successful Writing	8
Early Memories	9
Reflection	9

Unit 2 Picking Up Clues

Opportunities	10
Deciding What to Read	10
Helping You to Choose	12
Openings	13
Mindbenders Nicholas Fisk	13
Making Your Mind Up	16
Just As Long As We're Together Judy Blume	16
Agent Arthur's Jungle Journey Martin Oliver	17
Recording Your Reading	18
Recommending a Good Read	20
Organising Your Sentences	22
Organising Your Writing	22
Up and Up Shirley Hughes	23
Reflection	25

Unit 3 Making Words Work

Opportunities	26
Enjoying Poetry	26
Yellow Butter Mary Ann Hoberman	26
Unexpected Word Sounds	27
Hints on Pronunciation for Foreigners T.S.W.	27
Recognising Syllables	28
Words to Make Spells	30
Spell to Banish Fear Jeni Couzyn	30
Spell Poems	30
Unlocking the Meaning of Words	32
This is the Key of the Kingdom Traditional	32
The Door Miroslav Holub	33
Words to Bring Back the Past	34
Mum Dad and Me James Berry	34
Getting to Grips with Words	34
Giving everything a name – Nouns	35
Verbs	36
Reflection	37
Record Sheet for Units 1, 2 and 3	38

Unit 4 Mysterious Strangers

Opportunities	40
True or False?	40
'Kaspar Hauser' from *Mysteries* Tim Healey	40
Finding out for yourself	41
What Happens Next?	42
Sinful Sajid Hasnein Hussein	42
Story Shaping	48
Making Your Writing Interesting	48
Reflection	49

Unit 5 Imagine What Happened

Opportunities	50
Organising Your Description	50
The Eighteenth Emergency Betsy Byars	50
Writing in Paragraphs	51
Describing Places	52
'The Field' from *Jamaican Child* Errol O'Connor	53
'The Alley' from *Elidor* Alan Garner	53
Describing People	54
'Two-Bit Matthews' from *The Outsiders* S.E.Hinton	54
Choosing the Right Moment	56
The Describing Words	58
Adjectives All Around	58
When Did It Happen?	60

Contents

Past or Present?	60
'Night in the Garden' from *Animals At Night* Christopher Tunney	60
Responding to a Book	62
Five Things to Do with a Book	62
Keeping a reading log	62
Making a tape recording	63
Reading together	63
Illustrating a novel	64
Questioning a book	64
Reflection	65

Unit 6 Getting to Grips with Language

Opportunities	66
What is a Subject?	66
The Sentences Game	68
Language and Thought	72
Talking without Words	72
Developing an Alphabet	73
Making Up a New Language	74
Jabberwocky Lewis Carroll	74
Reflection	75
Record Sheet for Units 4, 5 and 6	76

Unit 7 Thinking About the Future

Opportunities	78
Play for Tomorrow	78
Survival of the Fittest Brian Keaney	78
Using the Exclamation Mark	87
Setting Out a Script	88
Operation Orpheus 1	90
The Threat to the Environment	90
Orpheus	92
The Future Tense	95
Reflection	95

Unit 8 Learning from Experience

Opportunities	96
A Story from Jamaica	96
Becky and the Wheels-and-brake Boys James Berry	96
Who's Who in the Story?	102
Granny-Liz	103
Shirnette	103
The Wheels-and-brake Boys	104
Mister Dean	104
What's Behind the Story?	105
Painting Pictures with Words	106
Writing Your Own Short Story	107
Starting Writing	107
Composing	110
Revising	110
Proof-reading	111
How to set out speech in a story	111
Publishing	111
Operation Orpheus 2	112
The Journey Down	112
Underground Worlds	114
Starting to Live Underground	116
Z for Zachariah Robert C. O'Brien	116
Working as a Team	116
Reflection	117

Unit 9 The World Around You

Opportunities	118
Pressure for Change	118
Poisoned Talk Raymond Wilson	120
Who Killed Cock Robin? Traditional	121
Operation Orpheus 3	122
Fears Underground	124
Signs of Life	125
Reflection	125
Record Sheet for Units 7, 8 and 9	126
Acknowledgements	128

Unit 1 Starting Out

This Unit gives you the opportunity to

- *remember events and write about them*
- *draft your writing in a simple way*
- *follow instructions*
- *talk about yourself*
- *work in a group*

A good way to start writing is to look at your own life. Everyone has memories. Some of these you use every day, for instance when you remember where you live! Other memories are not so easy to recall. When you read this piece of writing, you will see how an eleven-year-old girl describes some of her earliest memories.

My Memories

I think one of my earliest memories is of a young man called Simon who lived in the same block of flats as we did. He was a friend of my mum and dad when I was about ten months old. He picked me up, swung me round and put a daisy behind my ear.

A little while after that, when I was about eighteen months old, we had a new brown carpet and my parents had just finished decorating and had laid the carpet. They went into the kitchen to have a cup of tea. I found an opened tin of gloss paint and decided to paint the carpet with it. I don't think it would have mattered so much if the paint had been brown but it was white and really showed on the brown carpet.

I think my next memory was when we had just moved to a flat in Crystal Palace. I was about twenty months and I was standing in the garden with the grass reaching to just below my eyes.

Another thing I remember was when both my parents went to hospital because my little sister was being born. I was being looked after by my uncle and he took me out for a walk. I remember him holding my hand while I was walking along the wall.

My next memory is also in Crystal Palace. I was about four and my dad was making me and my sister a tree house. I was handing him the nails but

Learning to Remember

then he went inside for a cup of tea and leant the ladder he was using against a smaller tree. I got bored waiting for him so I climbed up it and hid in the tree till he came back. He came and took the ladder away without noticing I was there. So I waited till he started work again, then shouted, "Hello Daddy" and fell out of the tree. I cracked my head open on the corner of some bricks. I was crying and crying and my dad rushed to me and carried me indoors. He got blood all over his clothes. I had to go to the hospital and after the nurse asked me how I did it she said that girls shouldn't climb trees and I wouldn't talk to her at all again.

Emily, age 11

In a small group, talk together and decide about these points.

◆ Which of these memories do you think are good? Which are bad?

◆ Why do you think Emily particularly remembers these events?

◆ What kinds of things do people remember? Are the things that different people remember similar in any ways?

Tell your group about anything in your own life which Emily's memories have reminded you of.

Drawing a Time-line

If you look at the diagram below, you will see that it was drawn by Emily, too.

This diagram can be called a **time-line,** and it's a useful way of looking at events in your own life so far. It helps to decide which events have been most important to you, and to see when they happened.

1. Draw your own time-line. Mark on it up to twelve events from your life.

2. Share and talk about your time-line with someone else. Here are some questions that may help you when you consider each other's time-lines. What do the time-lines have in common (that is, what is to be found in both)? What are the differences?

When do *your* earliest memories start? Which of the other person's memories you have heard did you find the most interesting?

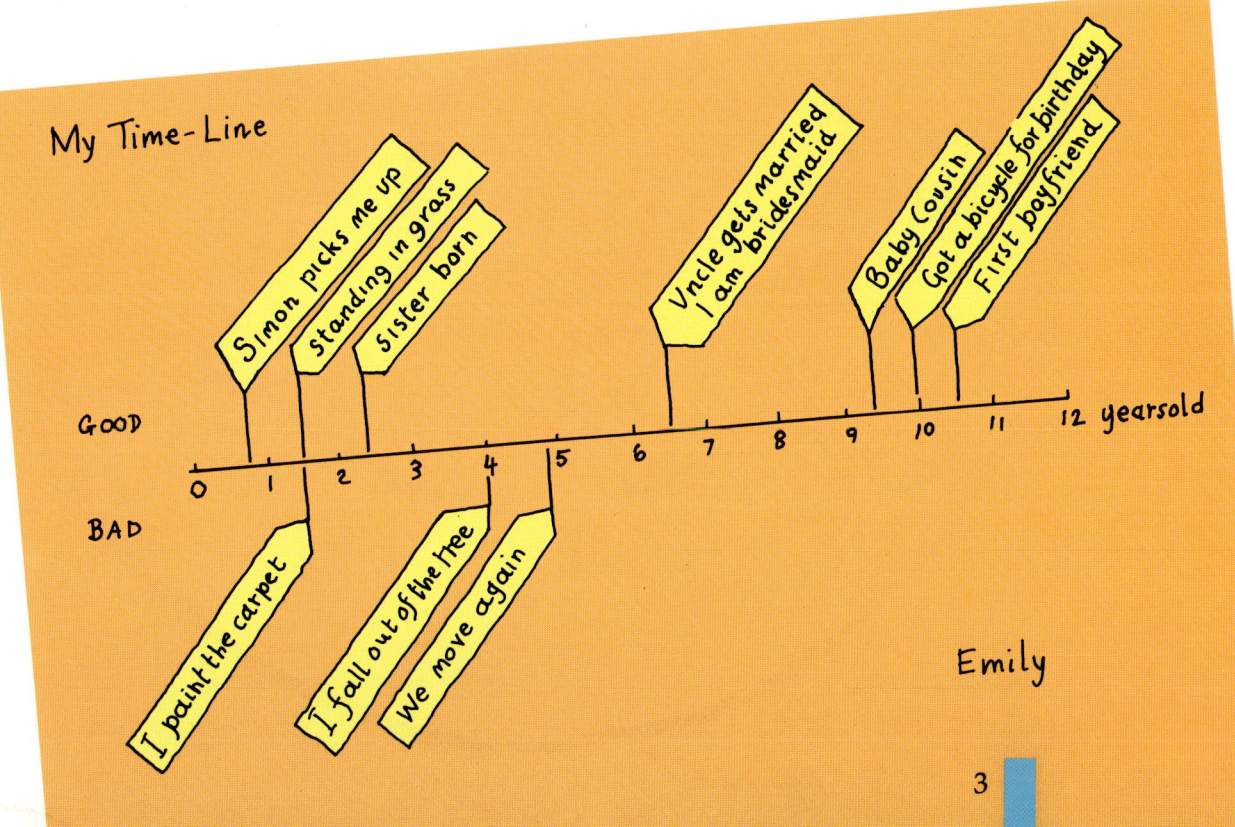

Learning to Remember

Centre of Attention

At each stage in your life you come into contact with different people. Some of these you see more often than others, some are more important than others.

This is a diagram drawn by Emily and shows the people in her life when she was eleven. In the circle nearest 'Me' (Emily) are the people closest and the most important to her.

1 Draw a Centre-of-Attention diagram like this for yourself as you are now. Draw another for a different time in your life. You may have to talk to your family about this to help you complete the second Centre-of-Attention diagram.

Successful Groupwork

You will already have had experience of working in pairs and in small groups. The better you can work as part of a group, the better your English is likely to become. This is because of the way people share ideas, speak and listen, when they are working together. From time to time in your English lessons you will try different ways of improving the way you work in a group.

When you do this, you will need to

◆ say what you think, give your opinion
◆ listen carefully to other people
◆ report back to the whole class

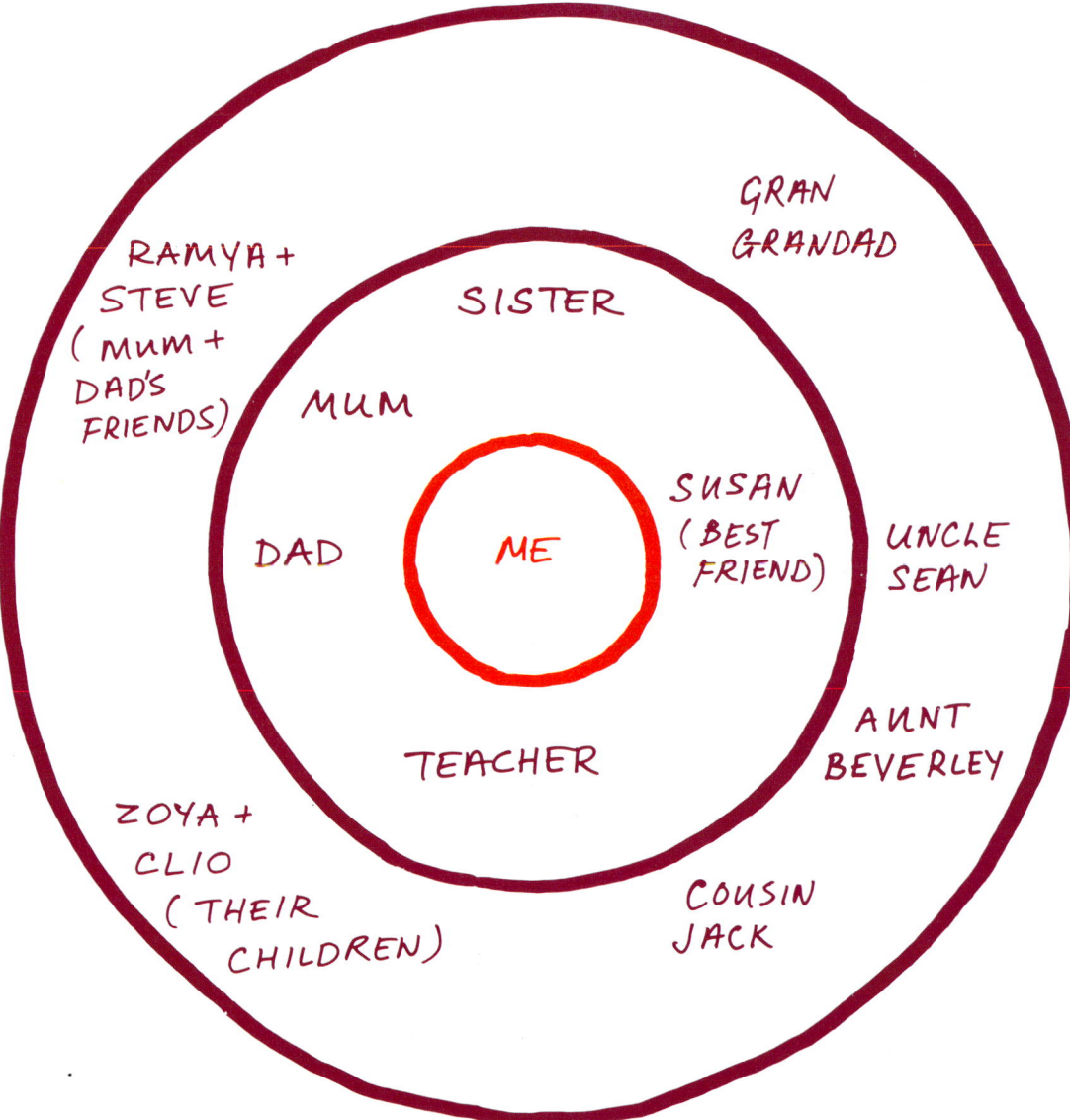

Learning to Remember

Remembering in detail

It is important to recall the details of your memories, and one helpful way of making your memories more detailed is to ask yourself the right questions.

1. On a separate piece of paper, imagine you were filling in this questionnaire. There is a heading and then important and useful questions to find out more <u>details</u>. Do this on your own or in pairs.

2. In small groups, compare your answers with those of the rest of your group. Choose one person to speak for your group and report back to the class.

3. In pairs, make a list with other headings from subjects like Celebrations and Holidays, for example Accidents and Friends. For each heading, make up at least two questions like the ones in the questionnaire.

4. In your group again, read out all the headings and questions you have made up. In your group choose the best ones from everybody's, and then answer them on your own.

The Memory Game

The Memory Game is a board-game with a difference. Play the game in a small group. Before you start you need to make a set of twelve Memory Cards. Each Memory Card begins with these words

> 'Describe and talk about – '

Cards look like this.

Memory Cards
Describe and talk about a really great moment in your life.

Memory Cards
Describe and talk about a day trip you have been on.

Memory Cards
Describe and talk about your last day at primary school.

1. Using the headings which you chose earlier (for activity 3 on this page), think of eleven more instructions to go on your Memory Cards. The questions in the questionnaire may help you to think of some instructions. Try and make them something which everybody will be able to talk about. Now turn over and play the game.

QUESTIONNAIRE • QUESTIONNAIRE • QUESTIONNAIRE

Celebrations

a) What was your favourite present ever?

b) Have you ever been given a present you did not want? If so, explain why.

c) Which Christmas, Diwali, Hannukah, Eid, New Year or other festival do you remember most? Why?

d) Have you ever been to a wedding? If so, whose was it?

Holidays

a) What is the most exciting holiday you have ever had? Where was it? Who were you with?

b) Have you ever had a holiday when something went badly wrong? If so what was it? How was it sorted out?

Learning to Remember

THE MEMORY GAME

RULES OF THE GAME

The game is played in groups of between 3 and 5. You will need counters and dice. You will need to decide on a time-limit for the game.

The object of the game is to talk in detail about your memories.

1. Players move around the board by throwing the dice.

2. If a player lands on a blue square s/he picks up a Memory Card and follows the instructions on that card. The card is then placed at the bottom of the pack.

3. If a player lands on a picture square s/he has to decide what the picture means to her/him and talk for at least thirty seconds about it.

4. If a player lands on a different coloured square the turn passes to the next player.

Learning to Remember

Successful Writing

Good writing doesn't often appear out of nowhere. It normally follows a period of thinking and rough work. This process is called **drafting.**

Throughout your English lessons you will be learning various drafting techniques. At the very least, writing involves these simple stages. There are more chances to practise your drafting in other units. The guide below takes you through these drafting stages.

STARTING WRITING

Deciding who you are writing for

Getting ideas

Planning

COMPOSING

Writing a rough draft

REVISING

Showing it to someone else and improving your writing

PROOF-READING

Checking your spelling and punctuation

PUBLISHING

Making a final draft

Successful Writing

Early Memories

1 Describe your earliest memories for the people in your new class.

Starting Writing

Decide who you are writing for.
Choose a number of your earliest memories. Make a list of all the things that go with each memory. You could do this using a spidergram like the one below. This shows Emily's memories. The arrows in the spidergram show how each event is connected.

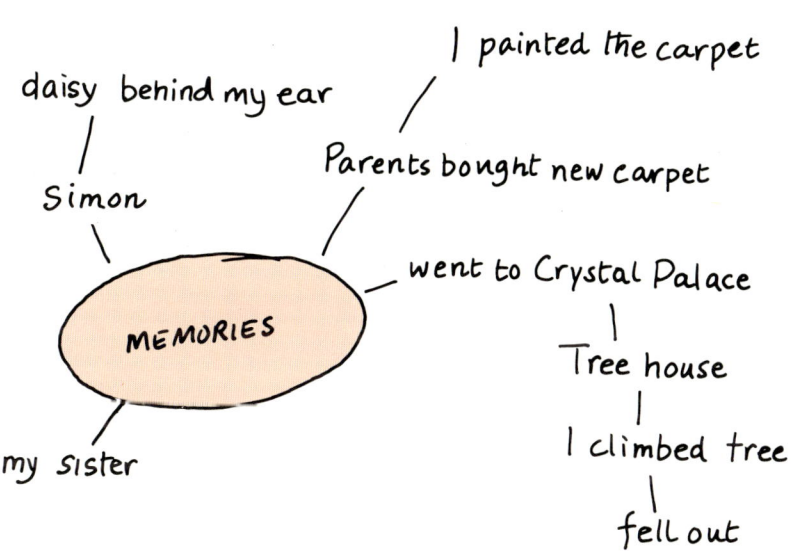

Composing

Do a rough draft. Think carefully about your sentences and the words you use.

Revising

Read your rough draft to someone in your group. Ask them how they think it could be improved.

Decide how you want to improve your writing. This might include one or all of these things:

- Changing the order of your writing
- Leaving something out
- Finding new ways of saying other things

Proof-reading

Check your spelling and punctuation.

Publishing

Decide how you want to present your final neat draft. Is it going to be handwritten or typed? You could make a class book or a wall display with illustrations.

2 In a small group read each others' writing. Talk about what happens in your descriptions. What do you think makes them interesting?

A display of your early memories, perhaps with photographs, will help your class get to know each other.

Reflection

In this Unit you have been practising how to

- describe an event
- ask and answer questions in groups
- follow instructions
- listen and respond to what has been read
- draft writing with help

Talk to your friends and your teacher about the things you have been doing in this Unit. Decide how much you have understood and how much progress you have made. Filling in Unit 1 of the Record Sheet on page 38 will also help you think about what you have done in this Unit and the knowledge you are gaining in your English lessons.

Unit 2 Picking Up Clues

This Unit gives you the opportunity to
- predict events
- read aloud confidently
- talk about what you have been reading
- keep a record of your reading
- present your ideas
- recognise and use simple sentences

Choosing a book is an exciting moment, but how do you decide on your next book when you are stuck for ideas and no-one around you can recommend a really good read? As a first step, you can find out quite a lot about a book from the picture on its cover. Secondly, does the title sound interesting? You can also look to see what the writing on the back of the book, which is called the **blurb**, tells you.

Deciding What to Read

1. In pairs, think and talk together about how you choose the books that you read.

   Follow this by studying these book covers carefully.

   Decide what you think each book might be about.

   Would you want to choose it? Explain your reasons carefully. Where else do you use a blurb or a cover picture to help you choose something?

2. Report your findings back to a group or to the rest of the class. Tell them what you have found out about the way covers and blurbs work.

Helping You to Choose

Many libraries use stickers to help young people choose books. For example, a book with a story about animals might have this sticker on the **spine**:

The spine is the backbone of a book. The pages are attached to it. Usually, too, it will carry the title and author's name on it.

1 In pairs, look at these stickers which are picture labels, and at the headings next to them. See if you can decide which picture label matches each heading.

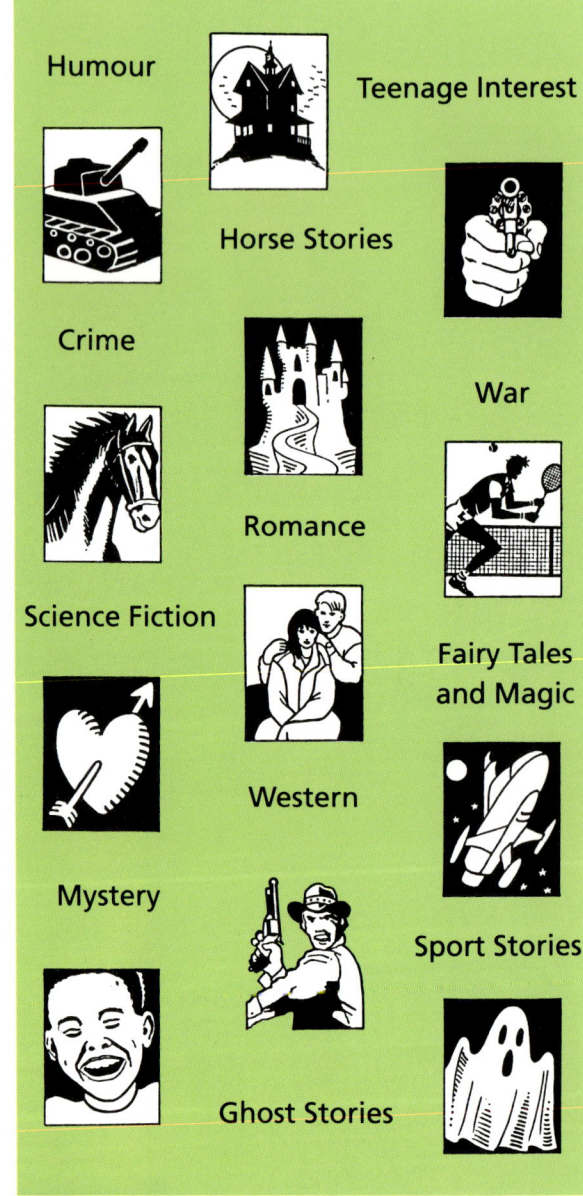

2 What other headings can you think of to describe different types of books? Often stories are a mixture of these different types of headings. What do you think the library can do then?

Make a list of any you think of. Draw your own pictures for them.

3 Choose a number of books from your school library and decide what headings you would put them under.

Helping You to Choose

Openings

Once you have decided to open a book, the first few pages will give you clues about what the rest of the story will be like.

1 In pairs, read and study the opening page of a story called *Mindbenders* written by Nicholas Fisk.

◆ Have you seen a first page like this before?
◆ What seems to be unusual about it?
◆ Why do you think you might enjoy a book in this style?
◆ The story continues on page 14. Before you turn over, can you work out who Vinny and Toby are? Can you work out what happened?

Now turn over. This is what follows.

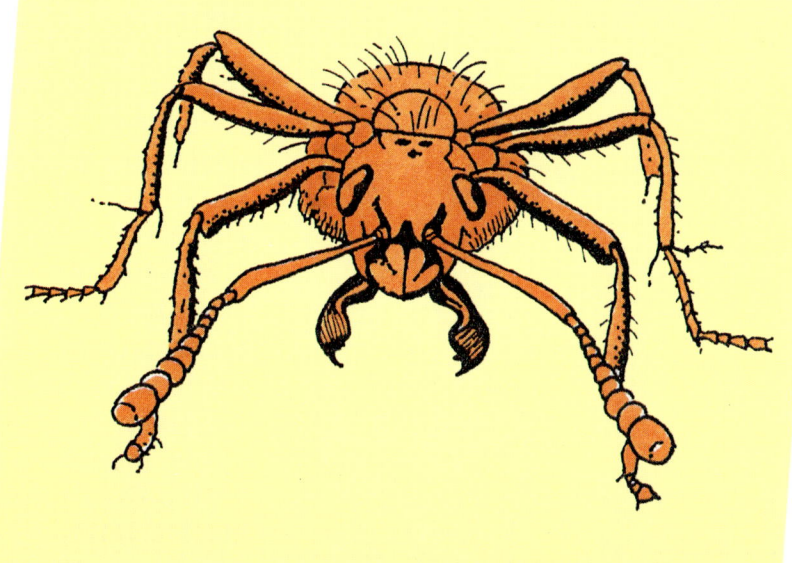

Helping You to Choose

Mindbenders

Vinny said, 'No, don't, we mustn't, it's cruel, it's mean.'

But her brother Toby saw the corners of her mouth twitch. 'Ah, come on,' he said. 'Do old Bloggs good. Wake him up.'

They were upstairs looking out of the window and down on the garden. It was sunny, hot, Bloggs lay on his favourite paving stone, legs stretched, golden eyes narrowed to slits. Happy fat black cat.

'Look at his bulging belly!' Toby said, 'Middle-age spread. He needs exercise. We'd be doing him a favour.'

'He's not middle-aged,' Vinny said.

'He is. You're nine, he's ten, I'm eleven. Bang in the middle.'

'Ten's not middle-aged for a cat,' Vinny said. She stared worriedly at Bloggs. You multiply a cat's age by seven, or is it five? Either way, she thought, I suppose Bloggs is getting middle-aged. How sad.

At that moment, Bloggs rolled over and lay on his back, with limp front paws dangling over his chest and his rear legs stretched out rigidly, like stilts. Even at this distance, you could see the smirk on his face. Vinny had to smile, then laugh.

'Go on!' Toby insisted.

'Well ...,' she said. The frown came back to her face, but a different frown, a frown of intense concentration. Her dark eyes became black, her lower lip pouted. 'Little brown mouse ...,' she murmured.

'Terrific, that's it, keep at it!' Toby whispered.

'*Little brown mouse, little brown mouse!*' Vinny repeated.

And there it was: a little brown mouse, sleek and plump! It sat on its haunches almost in front of Bloggs's nose. Its whiskers vibrated. It washed itself.

'Great, terrific, brill, genius!' Toby murmured.

At first, Bloggs saw nothing, He was too busy enjoying the sun. But then he rolled over, yawning – and glimpsed something small, brown, glossy and plump. A mouse! A mouth-watering, succulent mouse!

His sun-bathing position became a stalking crouch. His chin touched the warm paving stone. His shoulder-blades made two devilish humps, higher than his head. The tip of his tail twitched.

The mouse washed behind its ears with paws that moved as fast as an electric buzzer.

Helping You to Choose

Bloggs crawled forward on his belly, a centimetre at a time.

The mouse kept washing itself.

Vinny bit her lip and stared, fascinated.

Bloggs was within springing distance.

Toby rubbed his hands and stared, wide-eyed.

Bloggs bunched his muscles. He had only to spring, claws spread, hooked teeth ready to crunch shut –

'*Cancel!*' Vinny shouted.

And suddenly, there was no mouse.

       Nicholas Fisk

2 Still confused? In pairs, try to decide which of these statements are true and which are not:

The little brown mouse is not really there

Vinny and Toby are two cats

Bloggs is not really there

The little brown mouse appears and disappears

Bloggs is a cat

Vinny and Toby are adult humans

Vinny made the mouse appear

Toby was frightened of the mouse

3 Now turn back to the beginning of *Mindbenders*. After the first four lines there is a picture of an ant. Can you guess what this might have to do with the story?

4 Read what another eleven year-old wrote about the story.

> Vinny and Toby are two children. They have got a fat cat called Bloggs. One day their bossy aunt comes to stay. She brings them a strange present – an ants' nest in a case. When they stare into it, they find out that they can use the power of the ants to make amazing things happen.

Making Your Mind Up

1 In small groups, study two more openings. These are from *Just As Long As We're Together* by Judy Blume and *Agent Arthur's Jungle Journey* by Martin Oliver.

Just As Long As We're Together

"Stephanie is into hunks," my mother said to my aunt on Sunday afternoon. They were in the kitchen making potato salad and I was stretched out on the grass in our yard, reading. But the kitchen window was wide open so I could hear every word my mother and aunt were saying. I wasn't paying much attention though, until I heard my name.

At first I wasn't sure what my mother meant by *Stephanie is into hunks*, but I got the message when she added, "She's taped a poster of Richard Gere on the ceiling above her bed. She says she likes to look up at him while she's trying to fall asleep at night."

"Oh-oh," Aunt Denise said. "You'd better have a talk with her."

"She already knows about the birds and the bees," Mom said.

"Yes, but what does she know about boys?" Aunt Denise asked.

It so happens I know plenty about boys. As for hunks, I've never known one personally. Most boys my age – and I'm starting seventh grade in two weeks – are babies. As for my Richard Gere poster, I didn't even know he was famous when I bought it. I got it in a sale. The picture must have been taken a long time ago because he looks young, around seventeen. He was really cute back then. I love the expression on his face, kind of a half-smile, as if he's sharing a secret with me.

Actually, I don't call him Richard Gere. I call him Benjamin but my mother doesn't know that. To her he's some famous actor. To me, he's Benjamin Moore, he's seventeen and he's my first boyfriend. I love that name – Benjamin Moore. I got it off a paint can. We moved over the summer and for weeks our new house reeked of paint. While my room was being done I slept in my brother's room. His name is Bruce and he's ten. I didn't get a good night's sleep all that week because Bruce has nightmares.

Anyway, as soon as the painters were out of my room I moved back in and taped up my posters. I have nineteen of them, not counting Benjamin Moore. And he's the only one on the ceiling. It took me all day to arrange my posters in just the right way and that night, as soon as my mother got home from work, I called her up to see them.

"Oh, Stephanie!" she said. "You should have used tacks, not tape. Tape pulls the paint off the walls."

"No, it doesn't," I said.

"Yes, it does."

"Look ... I'll prove it to you," I said, taking down a poster of a lion with her cubs. But my mother was right. The tape did pull chips of paint off the wall. "I guess I'd better not move my posters around," I said.

"I guess not," Mom said. "We'll have to ask the painters to touch up that wall."

I felt kind of bad then and I guess Mom could tell because she said, "Your posters do look nice though. You've arranged them very artistically. Especially the one over your bed."

Judy Blume

Making Your Mind Up

A Mysterious Message

Agent Arthur was sitting in a small office of the Action Agency. But there wasn't much action going on. In fact, except for Arthur and his dog Sleuth, no one had walked through the door in weeks and weeks.

It was summer and Arthur had been left minding the office while his Uncle Jake was away on a top secret mission. His uncle was often away for weeks, months and sometimes years on end. Meanwhile, Arthur stayed put.

Arthur was reading a comic, and dreaming about having adventures like Uncle Jake, when CRASH. . . something hurtled through the window and whistled past his left ear. He dived for cover.

Ten seconds later, Arthur peered out from behind the desk. Papers were scattered everywhere. Among them was a half-brick. Sleuth sniffed the brick warily, while Arthur cautiously removed a piece of paper wrapped around it. He saw strange signs scrawled on it – the unmistakable symbols of the Agency Action Code.

What does the message say?

Making Your Mind Up

2 Choose two people in your group to read each passage aloud, one per passage. Choose another to make notes.

3 Decide what kind of book you think each one is going to be from the passage you have read and talk about the reasons for your decisions. (The pictures on pages 16 and 17 may help you get some ideas about this.)

   Jot down any clues you can find that tell you

   ◆ who the people are
   ◆ what might be going to happen

4 Make a note of what each member of the group thinks of the two openings. Choose a spokesperson, that is, one person to speak for your group, and report your findings back to the rest of the class.

Recording Your Reading

1 In a small group, talk about either the book you are reading at the moment or the last book that you read.

   Explain

   ◆ what kind of book it is
   ◆ what it is about
   ◆ what you thought of it

   From time to time in your English lessons you will be learning how to make a record of your reading so that you can get the most out of it. To start with, it is important to record what you read in a useful but simple way. A Reading Record chart like the one on the right helps you to think about the books you are reading and what you think of them. If you share your chart, your friends can use it too, to choose new books.

2 Copy out and complete this chart.

The Reading Record of	
Title of Book	Author
Just As Long As We're Together	Judy

Making Your Mind Up

Janice Menzies

me	Type	Comment	Date

3 Fill in the details of the last two books you have read.

You could draw a picture label like the ones on page 12 to show the type of book.

You could invent a star rating system to add to your comment section to show how much you liked the book.

4 In pairs, interview your school librarian about what s/he thinks makes a good read.

First, prepare a list of questions. These should include these points.

- ◆ what headings your school library uses
- ◆ whether your librarian gets any advice before choosing books for the library
- ◆ how your librarian would go about organising a display of books

Think of other questions about the way the library works.

You could tape record your interview.

Recommending a Good Read

A good read can be hard to find. It often helps if a friend or someone with similar interests to you can recommend a book. Here is a way to help someone choose what to read. It will also give you the opportunity to think hard about the books you have read.

1 To begin with, look back at your Reading Record. Choose from it the book which you really enjoyed the most. Follow these stages and recommend a book to someone in your class.

Stage 1

On your own, make a list of all the things you liked about the book you have chosen. You may not feel that you need to write down your notes at this stage, but remember the list will help you talk well about the book.

You need to be able to describe the story, say what it was about and why it was good. Your suggestion for a really good read will be a bit like the blurb (page 10) on the back of the book and the comments you made in your Reading Record will help you to think back.

Recommending a Good Read

Stage 2

Choose a partner who has not read the book you are going to describe. Try out what you are going to say on them.

Stage 3

Listen to your partner's comments on your recommendation. Talk to them about how you could improve the way you describe your choice.

Together, discuss the things you could do to make your talk more interesting. What sort of information does your partner, the listener, need to know about the book?

Was everything you said clear? Your partner can also give you one or two hints to help you improve the way you say things.

2 Now swap around and listen to his or her suggestions for a good read.

You might like to make a video or tape recording of students in your class giving their suggestions for a really good read.

You will need to decide

- which books you are going to include
- who is going to speak
- how you will organise the recording
- where you are going to record

Organising Your Sentences

When speaking, people leave short gaps in what they are saying as they go along so as

not to confuse the person they are talking to and

to breathe!

As you know, when writing you also need to leave 'gaps' between groups of words.

These 'gaps' are created by using punctuation marks like these. They allow you to make your meaning clear as you complete an idea and move onto the next one.

. (a full-stop)
! (an exclamation mark)
? (a question mark)

The words between the gaps are normally called **sentences**. As this course develops you will learn about the many different kinds of sentences which exist in English.

1 This is best done together. In pairs, look at these two pieces of writing.

   How many of the punctuation marks listed above can you find?

   There is one other punctuation mark in the passage. Can you see where it is? Find out what it is called.

   Which piece makes more sense and why?

A

Jenny and her younger brother Bill are walking their dog Fortissimo though the woods when they come upon a strange apparition where has it come from what is it trying to tell them Jenny and Bill become more involved with the Thing and more bewildered by it what can it be

B

Jenny and her younger brother Bill are walking their dog, Fortissimo, through the woods, when they come upon a strange apparition. Where has it come from? What is it trying to tell them? Jenny and Bill become more involved with the Thing and more bewildered by it. What can it be?

2 Can you think of any other ways in which speaking might be different from writing?

3 Find a piece of your own writing. Read it again. Are there any problems with understanding the meaning? If so, what are they? Now exchange your piece with your partner. Do you have any problems with each other's pieces?

   Listen again to your interview with your school librarian. Write out his or her answers to your questions. Do you think the librarian would have put anything differently, left anything out, or added anything if s/he had been writing and not speaking the answers? Can you find any examples?

Organising Your Writing

There are a few helpful rules in English. Some of the most important are about sentences.

Sentence Rule No. 1 All sentences start with a capital letter.

Sentence Rule No. 2 All sentences end with a punctuation mark that has a . in it, for example   . ! ?

Why do you need to know what a sentence is anyway?

There are several answers to this. Two answers are these.

1 It helps you to write clearly.

2 It helps you to read clearly.

Understanding and being able to write sentences is something that doesn't happen automatically. It is a bit like learning to speak when you are little.

Organising Your Sentences

1 In pairs, look at these cartoons. What are the differences between the ways the children are asking for food?

2 Stories for young children tend to use simple sentences. In pairs, look at this story for children, which continues over the page. There are no words, only pictures. Together, tell the story as simply as you can, by looking at the pictures.

23

Organising Your Sentences

3 When you have agreed what happens, write down your own version. Write your story for a child about the same age as Jo. Use simple sentences, starting with a capital letter and ending with a suitable punctuation mark. Remember to make sure that each of your sentences makes sense on its own.

The first part of this story has been done for you, to set you off.

Jo was playing with her bucket and spade. A bird came and sat beside her. The bird flew away. It joined lots of other birds.

Try reading your story to a young child.
Try reading other children's stories out loud.

Organising Your Sentences

Reflection

Up and Up Shirley Hughes

In this Unit you have been practising how to

- read and understand picture labels
- try to predict what type of story is in the book
- choose a reading book from the school library
- read aloud confidently
- listen to and talk about stories
- recognise that sentences have a beginning capital letter and a full stop, question mark or exclamation mark
- set out simple sentences to tell a story correctly

Talk to your friends and your teacher about the things you have been doing in this Unit. Decide how much you have understood and how much progress you have made. Filling in Unit 2 of the Record Sheet on page 38 will also help you think about what you have done in this Unit and the knowledge you are gaining in your English lessons.

Unit 3 Making Words Work

This Unit gives you the opportunity to

- *listen to and talk about poems*
- *read poems aloud*
- *listen to the different sounds words make*
- *write poems*

You will probably already have read and written a number of poems. Using this book, you will have the opportunity to enjoy a variety of different styles and types of poetry.

1 In pairs, read this tongue-twister aloud to each other. Start slowly and then see how fast and how confidently you can read it. It might be fun to do this one after the other, as a round. Which sounds do you find most difficult to say?

Yellow Butter

Yellow butter purple jelly red jam black bread
Spread it thick
Say it quick
Yellow butter purple jelly red jam black bread
Spread it thicker
Say it quicker
Yellow butter purple jelly red jam black bread
Now repeat it
While you eat it
Yellow butter purple jelly red jam black bread
Don't talk with your mouth full!

Mary Ann Hoberman

You could see how much of it you can learn off by heart.

In English, sounds are made by two kinds of letters, **vowels** and **consonants**.

Vowels are important to the sound that the middle part of words make. There are five vowels

a e i o u

All the other twenty-one letters are consonants, although the letter y can sometimes be used as a vowel.

Nearly all words have at least one vowel in them.

2 In pairs, look at and discuss the tongue-twister again. Do most of the words in it start with vowels or consonants?

3 Make a list of the words which you find most difficult to say. Look carefully at the consonants in the words in your list. Is it more difficult when you have a number of words which start with the same consonant?

4 Write out the alphabet and cross out the vowels. Watch your partner carefully as s/he says all the consonants in the alphabet. For which of them does s/he have to close the lips while speaking? How does the letter 'r' change when you say it as it is said on its own and when it is said at the start of a word like 'red'?

5 Find some other tongue-twisters like this or write your own. Try and learn them and then read one to a small group or the whole class. Can you write a tongue-twister that your teacher can't read?

Unexpected Word Sounds

1 People learning English find it difficult to work out how to say some words. Read this poem through to yourself. Stop to look up in a dictionary the meanings of any words you do not know.

Hints on Pronunciation for Foreigners

I take it you already know
Of tough and bough and cough and dough?
Others may stumble but not you,
On hiccough, thorough, lough and through?
Well done! And now you wish, perhaps,
To learn of less familiar traps?

Beware of heard, a dreadful word
That looks like beard and sounds like bird,
And dead: it's said like bed, not bead –
For goodness sake don't call it 'deed'!
Watch out for meat and great and threat
(They rhyme with suite and straight and debt.)

A moth is not a moth in mother
Not both in bother, broth in brother,
And here is not a match for there
Nor dear and fear for bear and pear,
And then there's dose and rose and lose –
Just look them up – and goose and choose,
And cork and work and card and ward,
And font and front and word and sword,
And do and go and thwart and cart –
Come, come, I've hardly made a start!
A dreadful language? Man alive!
I'd mastered it when I was five!

T.S.W.

2 In pairs, decide which words included in the poem look the same but sound different. Make a list of them.

3 Which words in this poem were new to you? Write them down with their meanings. Use a dictionary. The person who wrote this poem suggests that a five year-old would know how to say all these words. Do you agree?

Recognising Syllables

Some poems give readers clues to help them read them. For example, each line in the poem you have just read has eight small sounds in it.

It is helpful to know that these small sounds are called **syllables**. A syllable is the smallest part of a word that you can easily say. It nearly always has at least one vowel in it.

1. Rhymes or sports chants have very strong syllables in them. Choose one or two you know and clap as you say them, for example

Ma-ry ate jam
 1   2   3 4

Ma-ry ate jel-ly
 1   2   3 4 5

Ma-ry went home
 1   2   3   4

With a pain in her ... ?
 1   2   3   4   5

Al-gy met a bear
 1 2   3 4 5

The bear met Al-gy
 1   2   3   4 5

The bear grew bul-gy
 1   2   3   4 5

The bulge was Al-gy
 1   2   3   4 5

Recognising Syllables

2 See how many other chants you know. For example, there are skipping chants which need strong syllables.

3 In pairs, go through *Hints on Pronunciation for Foreigners*. Work out how each line is divided up into eight syllables.

4 Reading it aloud will help you study the poem, so take it in turns to read a line. Read it slowly and break up the words into their syllables. As you say each syllable, you could clap your hands to mark it out.

5 Try reading it together at normal speed, but with the syllables still easy to hear.

In the poem you can work out that 'know' and 'dough' have a similar sound because the last word in each pair of lines rhymes. Words that rhyme have the same sound for their last syllable.

1 Divide into small groups. How many one-syllable words can you think of that rhyme with 'know'? Make a list of them. Do the same for 'say' and 'make'.

2 Write a poem together that rhymes. Every line should have eight syllables, or as close to eight as you can make it! Each pair of lines should rhyme.

Start your poem with this line

I take it you already know ...

3 Read it aloud, with each member of your group taking at least one line.

Words to Make Spells

People have always been fascinated by the power of words.

Spell to Banish Fear

By the warmth of the sun
By the baby's cry
By the lambs on the hill
I banish thee.

By the sweetness of the song
By the warm rain falling
By the hum of grass
Begone.

                Jeni Couzyn

This spell has been written to 'banish' or get rid of fear. Each verse contains three things designed to make sure you are not afraid.

In pairs, decide

- why you think they have been chosen
- in what kind of voice you think the poem should be read

Jeni Couzyn used *Spell to Banish Fear* to encourage young people to write their own spells when she spent a day working in a school. Here are three of the poems they produced.

Spell to make the Tower of Pisa straight

By the wobble of the caterpillar
By the curl of a worm
By the bend in an old man's back
By the shape of a pencil
Let the tower of Pisa be straight!

By the curve of a head
By the spike of a dragon's tail
By the curve of my nose
Let the tower of Pisa be straight!

                Jack

Spell to get rid of a cough

By the sweet taste of lemon,
By the cold taste of ice-cream,
By the warm taste of tea,
By the fizzy taste of coke,
Begone cough.

By the plain taste of water,
By the sugary taste of icing,
By the sticky taste of bubble-gum,
By the sweet taste of raspberry,
Throat be good as new.

By the scream of a princess,
By the song of a bird,
By the croak of a frog,
By the roar of a lion,
My cough is cured.

                Sabrina

Spell to get rid of my nervousness

By the roar of a lion
By the fire of a dragon
By the howl of a wolf
By the teeth of a bear
Take away my nervousness.

By the spook of a ghost
By the laugh of a witch
By the darkness of a black wood
By the jaws of a shark
Begone nervousness.

                Louisa

Words to Make Spells

1. In small groups, decide which one of these spells you like most and why.

The words in these poems could be divided into two different groups.

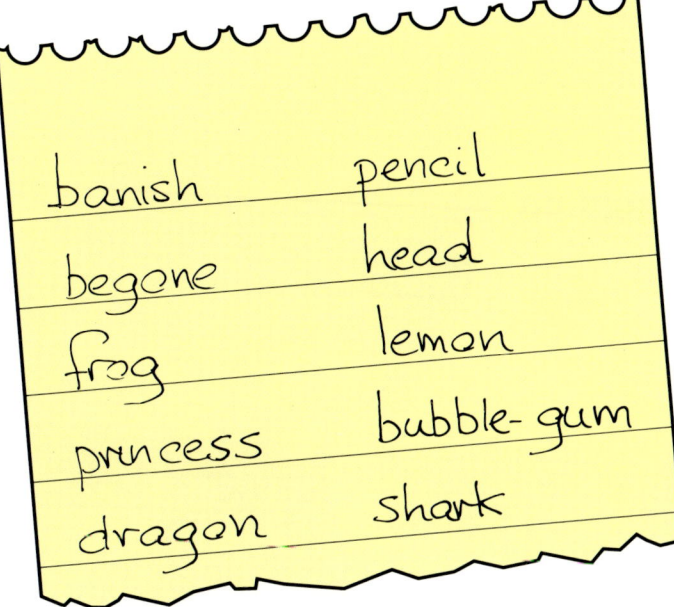

2. Which group makes you think of witches? Explain your reasons for this. Why have the words in the other group been chosen?
If the first set of words make you think of the magic and the words of the spell, what do the other set of words make you think of?

3. On your own, make up some spells suitable to be read to young children.

Starting Writing

Be clear who you are writing for. Talk about your ideas with a friend. Decide what kind of spell you would like to write. You could write spells to get rid of school, to end famine, to make you more attractive, to make you invisible or anything you can think of.

Make a list of all the words you are going to use to make your poem seem as if it might be spoken by a witch.

Think up some new words that are linked to the subject of your spell (like 'shape' and 'pencil' for the 'Tower of Pisa'). You could do this with a list or a spidergram like the one in Unit 1, Starting Out (see page 9).

Composing

Do a first draft for at least two different spells. Think about the words you will use and the structure of the spells.

Revising

Read your spells out to a friend. Get them to comment on the words you have used. Does your spell make sense to your friend? Will your spell be clear to young children?

Decide how you want to improve your spells. This might include one or all of these points.

◆ Changing the order of your writing

◆ Leaving something out

◆ Finding new ways of saying other things

Cross out and add all the changes you want to make on your rough draft.

Proof-reading

Check your spelling and punctuation. You could do this in small groups (use your dictionary). If you are making a lot of changes you may need to write out your spells again.

Publishing

Decide how you are going to present your final neat copy of the spells. You could also illustrate them. Think about and discuss with your friends how you can make your spells look like the ones you have been reading. You could wordprocess the spells.

4. Read your spells out in small groups. Which sound most like spells?

You might like to display the spells written by the class or make them into a book of spells.

Unlocking the Meaning of Words

In many poems there is no rhyme and no regular number of syllables in each line. But, even so, words can often form patterns as a result of their meaning.

In these two poems the words create an atmosphere and a pattern that is just as powerful as a strong rhyme or **rhythm**. Rhythm is the pattern of sounds made by words.

This is the Key of the Kingdom

This is the key of the kingdom:
In that kingdom there is a city.
In that city there is a town.
In that town there is a street.
In that street there is a lane.
In that lane there is a yard.
In that yard there is a house.
In that house there is a room.
In that room there is a bed.
On that bed there is a basket.
In that basket there are some flowers.
Flowers in a basket.
Basket on the bed.
Bed in the room.
Room in the house.
House in the yard.
Yard in the lane.
Lane in the street.
Street in the town.
Town in the city.
City in the kingdom.
Of that kingdom this is the key.

Traditional

Unlocking the Meaning of Words

The Door

Go and open the door.
Maybe outside there's
a tree, or a wood,
a garden,
or a magic city.

Go and open the door.
Maybe a dog's rummaging.
Maybe you'll see a face,
or an eye,
or the picture
of a picture.

Go and open the door.
If there's a fog
it will clear.

Go and open the door.
Even if there's only
the darkness ticking,
even if there's only
the hollow wind,
even if
      nothing
          is there,
go and open the door.

At least
there'll be
a draught.

Miroslav Holub
(trans. Ian Milner and George Theiner)

This is the Key of the Kingdom

- What is the smallest thing mentioned in the poem?
- Why is it important?
- What does the word 'key' make you think of?
- In what way is the poem like a mirror?
- Do you like it? Why? Why not?

The Door

- What do the sounds in this poem remind you of?
- Why do you think it is set out on the page as it is?
- What is the poet sure that there will be on the other side of the door? How can he be sure?
- What other things might be behind the door?
- What does the word 'door' make you think of?
- Do you like it? Why? Why not?

2 Either on your own or in pairs, write a poem called

'This is the key of my house', which uses some of the ideas you have been talking about.

Or

Write a poem called 'The door', starting with the same first line as the poem you have read. In it explore what might be behind your imaginary door.

Try to write as confidently as you can without worrying about whether your poem is like the ones you have read.

1 In groups, read and discuss these two poems. What do you think each poem is about? How do the words create a kind of pattern?

If you need more help use these further questions to guide you.

Words to Bring Back the Past

1. In pairs, read the poem *Mum Dad and Me* to each other. First, one of you should read it quickly to get a sense of its meaning. Then, the other can read it more slowly and look at the detail of the poem.

Mum Dad and Me

My parents grew among palm trees,
in sunshine strong and clear.
I grow in weather that's pale,
misty, watery or plain cold,
around back streets of London.

Dad swam in warm sea, at my age.
I swim in a roofed pool.
Mum – she still doesn't swim.

Mum went to an open village market
at my age. I go to a covered
arcade one with her now.
Dad works most Saturdays.

At my age Dad played
cricket with friends.
Mum helped her mum, or talked
shouting halfway up a hill.
Now I read or talk on the phone.

With her friends Mum's mum washed
clothes on a river-stone. Now
washing-machine washes our clothes.
We save time to eat to TV,
never speaking.

My dad longed for a freedom in Jamaica.
I want a greater freedom.
Mum prays for us, always.

Mum goes to church
some evenings and Sundays.
I go to the library.
Dad goes for his darts at the local.

Mum walked everywhere, at my age.
Dad rode a donkey.
Now I take a bus
or catch the underground train.

James Berry

2. Talk about *Mum Dad and Me*. These questions will help you discuss and enjoy James Berry's poem.

   What do you learn about the poet's mum and dad?

   What is different for James growing up in England compared with his mum and dad's youth?

   Which of the things mentioned about Jamaica do you think James feels most strongly about?

   Do you think he would have preferred to have grown up in Jamaica? Why? Why not?

3. On your own, write in any way you like about your parents' or guardians' life as they grew up. Compare their experiences with your own. Try to bring out any differences there may be between you and them. You may need to question them carefully.

   Start by jotting down things which are the same and things which are different.

   Write it just for yourself. You could write a story or a poem. Call on your teacher or a member of your family to help you if necessary. You could use a wordprocessor to help you in this activity.

Getting to Grips with Words

You don't need to know how an engine works to drive a car. But there are times when, if you know what a few important parts do, you can get it to work better. For many people language is a bit like the engine of a car.

Throughout your English lessons you will learn about how words work. Remember you do not need to become the sort of 'mechanic' who only enjoys taking things apart. You only need to learn how a few 'parts' of language work so that you can write, read and talk together better.

Words to Bring Back the Past

Giving everything a name – Nouns

When people first started to talk using what we recognise as 'language', they needed to give names to everything around them. The first words they used were probably **nouns**. 'Tree' is a noun. A noun is the name of a thing or a person. You will learn more about nouns in your English lessons.

1. You use nouns all the time without even thinking about it. Divide into small groups. Look at this basket of shopping.

How many of these things are nouns? Why?

2. Which of the things in this shopping basket would you want to have for your breakfast? Imagine one of your group had been doing the shopping. What would the shopping list have looked like?

Complete this list, changing the two items on it if they are not to your taste!

3. In your group, make a list of your favourite food. Are all the items on your list nouns? Why?

4. How many nouns can you see around the class? In pairs, suggest ideas and check that each one is the name of a person or thing.

In pairs, using only nouns, try to explain to each other

What you had for your breakfast

Where you were after school last night

What you like to do in your spare time

How successful were you?

35

Verbs

Just to give things names was not enough. Men and women needed to talk about what those things did! 'Fall' is a **verb**. It tells you what the tree does. Verbs are about actions. A verb shows you what things do and how people behave. You will be learning more about verbs in your English lessons.

Nouns and verbs together are two of the most important types of words.

1. In pairs, try to conduct a conversation or to explain something, using only verbs.

   How successful is it? Was it easier using just nouns (See 4 on page 35)?

2. Look at each of your breakfast shopping lists. Imagine you are now in the kitchen making breakfast. What could you do to eggs? You can fry them, scramble them, or even drop them!

   Tell the person you are working with how you would prepare all of the items on your list. For example: I would fry the eggs ...

All the words you have used like **fry**, **cook**, **cut**, **mix**, **break** are verbs.

There are other ways of understanding which words are verbs.

**A tree falls
is falling
fell**

**Jane falls
is falling
fell**

Verbs tell you what happens.

They also tell you when it happens.

Verbs

Reflection

In this Unit you have been practising how to

- *talk about and listen to poems*
- *take part in a group discussion*
- *read a poem aloud*
- *write a poem*
- *assemble ideas for a story or a poem on paper or a wordprocessor*
- *show that you can see more than one meaning in a poem*

Talk to your friends and your teacher about the things you have been doing in this Unit. Decide how much you have understood and how much progress you have made. Filling in Unit 3 of the Record Sheet on page 38 will also help you think about what you have done in this Unit and the knowledge you are gaining in your English lessons.

Record Sheet for Units 1, 2 and 3

Important: Your teacher will give you photocopied versions of these two pages so that you do not need to write in this book.

First of all, with a friend, talk about and decide what the short statements mean. Discuss what you have been practising in English and how much you have understood of what you have done.

Next to each statement there are three targets to aim for. This is what they mean:

I understand this and have practised it.

I have done this with help.

I feel able to do this again.

If you are not sure what a statement means or whether you can do what it says, discuss it with your teacher.

Put a tick under the target that you think best describes what you can do. If you are in doubt, please ask for help.

Name of Student

I can

Unit 1
- describe an event in a group
- ask and answer questions in a group
- follow instructions
- listen and respond to what has been read
- draft writing with help

Unit 2
- read and understand labels
- predict events in a story
- choose a reading book from the school library
- read stories aloud confidently
- listen to and talk about stories
- recognise that sentences have capital letters and full stops/question marks etc.
- set out simple sentences in a story correctly

Unit 3
- listen to and talk about poems
- take part in a group discussion
- read a poem aloud
- write a poem
- assemble ideas for a story or a poem on paper
- assemble ideas for a story or a poem on a wordprocessor
- show ability to see more than one meaning in a poem

Record of Achievement in English

			Other Comments

Thinking Back

- Which is the best piece of work that you have done so far? Why do you think it was particularly successful?
- Which of the activities in the last three units did you enjoy most?
- What have you found out about English that you did not know before?
- Was there anything you did not understand and would like more help with?

Thinking Forward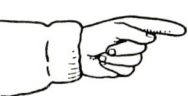

- Where do you think you need to improve most? What can you do to help you do so?
- What kind of activities can you suggest to your teacher that you could do as extra work?

Unit 4 Mysterious Strangers

This Unit gives you the opportunity to

- *read for information*
- *use reference and other information books*
- *predict events in a story*
- *give opinions*
- *write a story with a strong ending*

Reference books make interesting reading! They can set your imagination working just as a poem, play or story can.

1 Study this piece from a book about mysteries.

Kaspar Hauser

On Whit Monday in 1828 a strange boy was seen lurching along a street in the town of Nuremberg, Germany. He was gazing around in bewilderment. He spoke only in grunts, though one sentence came out clearly: "I want to be a soldier like my father."

When offered a pencil, the boy wrote his name: Kaspar Hauser. Kaspar was carrying a mysterious letter. It hinted that his father had been a cavalry officer and continued, "if you will not keep him you must strike him dead".

Kaspar behaved very oddly. He would sit for hours gazing emptily into space, and ate only bread and water. Anything else made him sick. He picked things up between thumb and forefinger, as if he did not know how to use his hands. Mirrors puzzled him. He was terrified of strong light and preferred darkened rooms. One man wrote, "he seemed like a creature from outer space."

Kaspar became a celebrity. People came from all over Germany to see him. A kindly local teacher took him in and taught him to read, write and draw pictures. His memory stirred and he spoke brokenly about events from his past.

Kaspar said he had been kept locked up in darkness for years. A dark figure had brought him food and water, and sometimes the water was drugged. One day the man had taught him to write his name and speak his one sentence. Then, after a drugged sleep, Kaspar found himself walking in dazzling daylight, apparently free.

All Germany buzzed with rumours and the case became famous throughout Europe. But one night in October 1829 the teacher's sister came home late. There was a trail of blood leading down from the hall to the cellar. There lay Kaspar. He had been brutally attacked. Blood was seeping from his forehead where a savage blow had been struck. "Man," he muttered, "man!"

But he did not die. As he recovered, he described his attacker as darkly clothed, with a silk mask and leather gloves. The case was becoming more fantastic. Who was the "man" who wanted him dead?

Four years later, Kaspar had been moved to the town of Ansbach under a new guardian. He had become solitary and thoughtful. And one day in December 1833 fate took another dark turn.

Kaspar went for a walk alone in the park. When he came back he was staggering. Blood was gushing from deep stab wounds in his lungs and liver. Kaspar gasped out his story. A tall stranger had lured him to the park promising to explain his past. When Kaspar arrived, the man offered him a wallet. As Kaspar reached for it, the knife was plunged into his breast.

Kaspar died three days later. His death shocked Europe. Some people were convinced that he must have been the unwanted son of some nobleman, perhaps even a member of the royal family. But there was no evidence for it. A memorial still stands in Ansbach park, bearing the inscription "Here, one unknown was murdered by another." Kaspar's dark secret died with him.

from *Mysteries*, Tim Healey

True or False?

2 Divide into small groups and read the piece about Kaspar Hauser again. Talk together particularly about the information given in this piece of writing.

3 Which of these statements do you agree with?

Which might be true? Which are false? Decide what you think about each one.

Kaspar Hauser was a cavalry officer

Kaspar Hauser was a creature from outer space

Kaspar Hauser had been held prisoner for many years by a wicked witch

Kaspar Hauser pretended he had lost his memory

Kaspar Hauser used to eat meat secretly

Kaspar Hauser was really a ghost

Nobody knows who Kaspar Hauser was

Kaspar Hauser was really a prince

Kaspar Hauser was killed because he knew something dangerous

Kaspar Hauser was just an ordinary boy

4 What was mysterious about Kaspar? Make a list of everything you can think of.

5 What explanations can you think of for this strange story?

Finding out for yourself

Most libraries have a separate reference section. There you can find dictionaries, encyclopaedias, computer equipment and reference books. To find out more about a mystery like the one you have been reading, go to the reference section.

1 Find out how to use an encyclopaedia or the reference books in your school library. Also, find out how to use any computer equipment you may have to give you the information you want.

2 Who were

Houdini?

Uri Geller?

Joan of Arc?

Rasputin?

Mata Hari?

3 Are there any other mysterious people or events that you have heard of or that interest you?

4 Working on your own, find out about one of the people in the list or one of your own choice. Give a short talk to your group or class. Make a list of the questions you need to ask the librarian. Remember, you need to find out the right information. What were his or her special powers? What was unusual about him or her as a person? Make notes that will help you in your talk. Brief words and phrases will outline the information you will need to explain in your talk.

5 In pairs or small groups, make a class pamphlet about mysterious people. (Remember to illustrate it.)

What Happens Next?

1 Read this story. It was written by a school student about another unusual boy. The story has been stopped at a number of important moments. See if you can guess what happens next, without turning over.

Sinful Sajid

Sajid had never been normal. He told me a lot of things about himself. When he moved into our neighbourhood crazy things started to happen, like he could just think of something and it would happen. I didn't believe him so he showed me …

"See that bottle on that rubbish bin," he said, pointing to an empty coke bottle somebody had left sitting on top of the black rubbish bin in the corner.

"Yeah," I said.

"Watch."

He sort of squinted his eyes like someone looking through a dirty window. The bottle toppled off the bin and shattered on the pavement.

What Happens Next?

"Anyone can do that," I told him, though I wasn't sure if I could. I thought he must have used some sort of trick, so I went on: "if you're so smart why don't you make all the pieces of glass jump back in the bin like a video film?"

"Can't," he said, "but I can do something much better than that. See that big bird in the air?"

A big crow was flying over Mr Johnson's house. Sajid stared at the old crow and started squinting at it and the old crow just stopped in midair like it had been shot. Then it dropped straight down and landed on Mr Johnson's hedge. It sat there, flapping its wings like crazy, flapping fit to burst and not daring to fly back in the air in case Sajid squinted at it again. That poor old crow didn't know what hit it.

"Fantastic!" I shouted as loud as I could. "You did that? You really did it?"

Sajid looked smug. "I can think things to people, too, you know," he boasted. "I can think things to you, or teachers or even anybody. But don't worry, I won't think anything to you, Jon. You and I are going to be friends," he said, without asking for my opinion.

But that was fine with me. Sajid seemed like fun. I took Sajid to meet the gang. It was near the end of the summer holidays and we were all going to play football in the park.

Sajid greedily wanted to be the leader, rather than let Tommy Glover. Tommy was quite big compared with Sajid but Sajid insisted. Then Glover went up to Sajid and said, "Who's the oldest – you or me? Who's the toughest – you or me?" And that was when big Glover made a big mistake: he punched Sajid to the floor!

Sajid got up in a rage but he did not strike back; he just squinted at Glover. And then I said to myself, "Oh now Sajid must be thinking something horrible."

2 What do you think happened to Glover? Decide before you turn over.

43

What Happens Next?

Just at that moment there was a sound like a slap at Glover's face. His left cheek went flat, lining up with his nose and a big bruise was formed on it. It was as if an invisible rock had hit against his cheek. He went red with pain and tears came rushing through his eyes as if a giant water pipe had burst and let water rush out through them. He ran in all directions like a crazy horse.

Sajid turned round like a snake and everybody took one step back and froze. He said, in a calm voice, "Don't be afraid, guys. I won't hurt you. After the game I'll treat you all." Everybody gave a fake smile like a lady at a bank. "Right, me and Jon against you two, okay?" And then everybody nodded an agreement. James and Anthony knew they had no chance against us two but they didn't argue.

Sajid and Anthony took kick off. Sajid fouled four times but no-one argued. Then Anthony scored one goal. Sajid didn't like it. So he made Anthony say it was no goal.

After the game he treated us like he said. He took us to the corner shop which had everything from sweets to a lady's handbag. He picked up a handful of chocolate bars and put them on the counter and then picked up another handful. Now there were about fifteen chocolate bars on the counter. The man looked at Sajid and said, "Are you going to buy them son? And if you are you better tell me where you got the money" and then picked up the telephone and dialled 999.

Sajid started to squint his eyes again and after about two seconds the person at the counter slammed down the telephone receiver with the look of a dead snake on his face, eyes wide as they could stretch. He turned round and went through the back door. We all looked at Sajid in shock and in confusion and fear.

When I got home mum asked me how did I get along with our new neighbour. I replied,

3 What do you think the writer said to his mum? Decide what you would have said.

What Happens Next?

"Well he is a bit strange; he can just think of something and it would happen."

My dad said, "He is a bit weird, I agree with you. Anyway, let's get one thing straight: he is not normal, so me and your mother have decided that you should not hang around with him."

I felt quite happy and a bit sorry because Sajid really seemed fun, although he was very bad-tempered at times.

The next day I woke up at eight o'clock and got dressed. It was the first day of school and seemed fun. When the school assembly finished we went to our classes as usual. It was English; we had Mr Norton. Mr Norton caught Sajid playing around and that was when Mr Norton made his big mistake: he insulted Sajid as much as he could. Sajid said to himself, "I'll teach you a lesson, Norton." And then he ran out of the class.

At home time he was waiting by the exit. Mr Norton went out slowly through the school gates. As he did Sajid started to squint his eyes and Mr Norton accelerated and smashed right into another car. It was just like it is on TV. I could not believe it.

Then Sajid came up to me and said, "Come on. You are going to meet my parents, aren't you? Come on."

I felt scared and frightened by Sajid. I was shaking all over. I had this cold feeling down my spine. I was walking in all directions. My brain felt as if there was a hole in the back of my skull and all the fear of the world was creeping into my brain and body through that hole. My brain was doing all sorts of different things which I did not want to happen.

But after a couple of minutes I felt better and I was standing on the porch. Sajid rang the bell. After a while his mum opened the door. Sajid went into the living room and switched on the telly. Then his dad came in. Sajid looked up and said to his dad, "Kneel down and lick my boots."

4 What do you think Sajid's dad did next? What would your dad do if you spoke to him like this? How do you think this story is going to end? Now read the ending.

What Happens Next?

His dad did just that!

Then after a while I said to Sajid, "I want to go home," but it was no use. He simply said, "No, not yet."

And then his little baby sister, Joan, started to scream and cry and that got on Sajid's nerves. So he got in a rage and said to his mother, who was just about to go upstairs, "I'm going to shut her up."

He went upstairs and was just standing over her cot when a gush of wind swept him away towards the window and there was a loud scream, like the whistle of a steam engine. Sajid went flying through the window. His mother looked at the broken window and then at her baby daughter. She went towards Joan and said, "Oh God, not another one!"

Hasnein Hussein

What Happens Next?

5 In groups, discuss the ending of the story. What do you think happened to Sajid? Why? What do you think Sajid's mum meant by, 'Oh God, not another one!'?

Did you think it was a good ending? If not, how would you have written it to make it better?

Story Shaping

Writing a good ending to a story is one of the most difficult things to learn. You will find it easier to do if you have planned your story carefully and haven't allowed it to ramble on! What do you think of the ending of *Sinful Sajid*? Explain why you think it was good or bad. What do you think makes a good ending to a story?

1 Look at the way Hasnein might have planned his story.

> Sajid moves in
> ↓
> The coke bottle
> ↓
> The crow
> ↓
> Glover and Sajid
> ↓
> The football game
> ↓
> The corner shop and the chocolate bars
> ↓
> First day at school and Mr Norton's accident
> ↓
> Sajid's dad licks his boots
> ↓
> Sajid is blown out of the window

2 In pairs, look through the whole story, and decide how many times Sajid uses his unusual powers.

This story is, in fact, like many traditional stories about a person with magical powers. The main character

- arrives in the area
- is then involved in a number of events with other characters
- finally comes to a sticky end!

It has a clear beginning, middle and ending and is the kind of story that you could easily write. It is up to the writer to decide how long the middle is.

Making Your Writing Interesting

As well as having a good plot or story, Hasnein has tried to keep his readers interested by the way he has described things.

1 Have a look at these examples:

> It was as if an invisible rock had hit against his cheek.

> Tears came rushing through his eyes as if a giant water pipe had burst and let water rush out through them.

> The person at the counter slammed down the telephone receiver with the look of a dead snake on his face, eyes wide as they could stretch.

2 How do the words in these descriptions help you to picture what is going on? Pick out any other examples of descriptions like these. Do you find them helpful? Which do you think is the most effective one?

3 Plan and write a story about a mysterious stranger for someone of your own age. Follow the stages on the opposite page.

Story Shaping

Starting Writing

Be clear who you are writing for. Talk about your ideas with a friend. Choose the kind of stranger you want to have in your story. She or he could be like the ones you have read about in this unit. They might have special gifts, like being able to make spells or have magic wishes. Make a list of words describing your stranger.

Decide where you are going to set your story. You could draw a map to help you think. Is your story going to involve you and your friends or is it going to be something completely different? A spidergram like the one in Unit 1, Starting Out (see page 9) may help you to think out the story.

How is it going to end? At this stage you may have a number of possible endings. Talk these through with a friend. Do a plan of your story showing the main things that are going to happen. You could set your plan out like the one in the story shaping section on page 48.

Composing

Using your plan of events, write your story out as a first draft. Try to include descriptions of key moments like those you have been reading. Picture your characters in as interesting a way as possible.

Revising

Share your story with a friend. Get them to comment on the beginning, middle and end of the story. Does your story make sense? Does everything happen in a clear order? Read your story to yourself and think about how you could improve it.

Decide how you are going to improve your writing. This might include one or all of these points.

- Changing the order of your writing
- Leaving something out
- Finding new ways of saying things

On your rough draft, cross out and add all the changes you want to make. If you are making a lot of changes you may need to write out the story again.

Proof-reading

Check your spelling and punctuation. Use a dictionary. You could do this in small groups. You may like to ask your teacher to point out some words to look at.

Publishing

Decide how you are going to present your final neat copy of the story. You could wordprocess the story.

You could illustrate and display your stories or make a class book of stories. Read your stories out to each other. Which are the most exciting?

Reflection

In this Unit you have been practising how to

- take part in a group presentation
- express opinions clearly
- use information books and equipment in the school library
- make a list of questions to help you select a reference book
- predict events in a story
- talk about setting and characters in a story
- show that you understand that stories have a beginning, middle and end
- write a story with a clear beginning, middle and end
- use a dictionary to check for spelling
- discuss the organisation of your writing as you draft it

Talk to your friends and your teacher about the things you have been doing in this Unit. Decide how much you have understood and how much progress you have made. Filling in Unit 4 of the Record Sheet on page 76 will also help you think about what you have done in this Unit and the knowledge you are gaining in your English lessons.

Unit 5 Imagine What Happened

This Unit gives you the opportunity to

- *recognise how paragraphs can be used*
- *read examples of description*
- *understand that description is helpful*
- *recognise and use adjectives*
- *understand how the past and present tenses can be used*
- *keep a reading log*
- *prepare a class presentation*
- *tape record a story*
- *choose a reading book for your own work*

All stories contain description – of places, of people and of what happens. There are many different ways in which this description can be organised.

1 Read and study this opening to a well-known book by Betsy Byars called *The Eighteenth Emergency*.

2 In pairs, look carefully at the first twenty-three lines of the book. They are split into four clear paragraphs.

The Eighteenth Emergency

The pigeons flew out of the alley in one long swoop and settled on the awning of the grocery store. A dog ran out of the alley with a torn Cracker Jack box in his mouth. Then came the boy.

The boy was running hard and fast. He stopped at the sidewalk, looked both ways, saw that the street was deserted and kept going. The dog caught the boy's fear, and he started running with him.

The two of them ran together for a block. The dog's legs were so short he appeared to be on wheels. His Cracker Jack box was hitting the sidewalk. He kept glancing at the boy because he didn't know why they were running. The boy knew. He did not even notice the dog beside him or the trail of spilled Cracker Jacks behind.

Suddenly the boy slowed down, went up some stairs and entered an apartment building. The dog stopped. He sensed that the danger had passed, but he stood for a moment at the bottom of the stairs. Then he went back to eat the Cracker Jacks scattered on the sidewalk and to snarl at the pigeons who had flown down to get some.

Inside the building the boy was still running. He went up the stairs three at a time, stumbled, pulled himself up by the banister and kept going until he was safely inside his own apartment. Then he sagged against the door.

His mother was sitting on the sofa, going over some papers. The boy waited for her to look up and ask him what had happened. He thought she should be able to hear something was wrong just from the terrible way he was breathing. "Mom," he said.

"Just a minute. I've got to get these orders straight." When she went over her cosmetic orders she had a dedicated, scientific look. He waited until she came to the end of the sheet.

"Mom." Without looking up, she turned to the next page. He said again, *"Mom."*

Organising Your Description

Writing in Paragraphs

A **paragraph** is a group of sentences. Each paragraph starts on a new line.

1. On your own, decide what each of the four paragraphs describes. Draw four simple pictures of what is in each paragraph.

2. Which of these descriptions do you think best fits each of these four paragraphs?

   A A boy and a dog are running hard along a block.

   B Pigeons rise up in alarm. A dog comes running out of an alley followed by a boy chasing it.

   C A boy stops running and goes into a building. His dog remains outside for a moment.

   D A boy is running fast. He seems nervous and is looking around him. His dog runs after him.

3. Make your own title for each of the four paragraphs.

4. In pairs, think about how the beginning of *The Eighteenth Emergency* is like one or all of these things:

   ◆ The first few minutes of a film
   ◆ The first few minutes of a new television series or play
   ◆ One of the television adverts that tells a story

5. Talk about how these four opening paragraphs describe the people and places in the story and how they get you interested.

6. In pairs, look carefully at the fifth and sixth paragraphs. Both of them continue to describe what the boy is doing. Who is the new person introduced in the sixth paragraph?

7. Look at the last two paragraphs. One has Benjie thinking hard, then telling his mother that someone is trying to kill him. The other has Benjie wandering into the room with his mother trying to find out what is wrong. Decide which is which.

8. What do you think of the opening of this story? Did this opening of a book make you want to read on? Explain your answer. What made the opening of the story interesting?

9. Why does Betsy Byars not tell us the boy's name at the start? Why do you think she doesn't tell us that Benjie thinks he is going to be killed until the end?

10. In a small group, talk about the passage and decide what you think is going to happen

    ◆ in the next paragraph
    ◆ by the end of the chapter

"I'm almost through. There's a mistake some –"
He said, "Never mind." He walked heavily through the living room and into the hall. He threw himself down on the day bed.

His mother said, "I'm almost through with this, Benjie."

"I said, 'Never mind.'" He looked up at the ceiling. In a blur he saw a long cobweb hanging by the light fixture. A month ago he had climbed on a chair, written UNSAFE FOR PUBLIC SWINGING and drawn an arrow to the cobweb. It was still there.

He closed his eyes. He was breathing so hard his throat hurt.

"Benjie, come back," his mother called. "I'm through."

"Never mind."

"Come on, Benjie, I want to talk to you."

He got up slowly and walked into the living room. She had put her order books on the coffee table. "Sit down. Tell me what's wrong." He hesitated and then sat beside her on the sofa. She waited and then said again, "What's wrong?"

He did not answer for a moment. He looked out of the window, and he could see the apartment across the street. A yellow cat was sitting in the window watching the pigeons. He said in a low voice, "Some boys are going to kill me."

Betsy Byars

Understanding Paragraphs

In the opening of *The Eighteenth Emergency*, the story starts with a bang and we begin to learn about Benjie and some things about his life. Betsy Byars uses paragraphs to tell us something new, about Benjie, his surroundings and what is happening.

All stories are divided up into paragraphs. If they were not, they would be very difficult to follow.

There is no simple way of saying what a paragraph is. From this extract you can see that here they show you different views of Benjie and make you want to read on to the next one.

Here are some ways of explaining what paragraphs are.

A paragraph is a group of sentences that are linked together (for example, in the paragraph where Benjie is thinking hard before deciding to tell his mother that someone is trying to kill him).

A paragraph is a group of sentences that move a story on (for example, in particular in the second paragraph in this extract).

A paragraph describes a new place or a new person in a story.

Throughout your English lessons you will learn about different types of paragraphs.

Describing Places

There are many different ways of writing about places.

1 Read these two descriptions of places.

The Field

The field itself was a long way from home. It was downhill all the way. The field was in a wide, open space. For miles it was green, with trees that rocked from left to right in the midday breeze. There were plants of different types, such as potatoes, tomatoes, and the long green leaves of tobacco. A river divided the wide field into two halves. Footpaths could be seen all around; sometimes they divided a field into sections. Trees of fruits, mangoes, breadfruits and grapes were on the gently sloping hills. Tall, fresh green grass surrounded them, but the cows that ploughed the fields would trample over it as they ate in the evenings.

from *Jamaican Child*, Errol O'Connor

Understanding Paragraphs

2 In pairs, answer these questions.

- Where do you think this field might be? Which words suggest this to you?
- What do you learn about the shape of the field? Make a simple plan or map including what you can work out. Compare your plan with other people's in the class.

The Alley

They were in an alley that ran between loading bays and store-houses lit by unshaded bulbs: the kerb was low and had a metal edge, and there was the smell of boxwood and rotten fruit. Fans pumped hot stale air into the children's faces through vents that were hung with feathers of dirt.

Beyond the alley they came to a warren of grimy streets, where old women stood in the doorways, wearing sacks for aprons, and men in carpet slippers sat on the steps. Dogs nosed among crumpled paper in the gutter; a rusty bicycle-wheel lay on the cobbles. A group of boys at the corner talked to a girl whose hair was rolled in brightly coloured plastic curlers.

from *Elidor,* Alan Garner

- What colours come into your mind as you read it?
- Do you think the writer of this piece knows the place he is describing? On what do you base your opinion?
- Why do you think this description was written? What sort of book do you think this is from?

1 Answer these questions, still in pairs.

- In this description, a group of young people in a city have left the safety of roads they know and are exploring a different area. Decide what kind of atmosphere you think the alley seems to have. Give examples of words which make you think this.
- Why do you think this description was written? What sort of book do you think this is from?
- Are there any words you don't know? If so, look them up in a dictionary.
- Everything which Alan Garner chooses to include is made individual. For example, the kerb is not just a kerb it is a low kerb with a metal edge. What other examples of this kind of detail can you find in the passage? Make a list of them.
- You can see the dirt and almost hear the people talking and the dogs rustling the paper with their noses. This is one way in which a writer makes a description come alive. What other sense does Alan Garner appeal to? What does it make you think of?

2 In pairs or on your own, choose an area of your school or somewhere near to it and try to describe it for a friend.

When you are looking at the place you have chosen, study it carefully, allowing your eyes, ears and nose to take it in. Make a list of words that could describe your area.

3 Write a paragraph describing your special place. You could write your description as if it came from

- a murder story set in your school
- a love story set in your school

Describing People

Often paragraphs are useful when you want to single out a particular character in a story and describe him or her. They are especially helpful when you want to introduce a new person.

In a novel by S. E. Hinton called *The Outsiders*, there is a gang of young people. Each of them is different and as they are introduced we are given brief descriptions to help us to remember them.

Two-Bit Matthews

Two-Bit Matthews was the oldest of the gang and the wise-cracker of the bunch. He was about six feet tall, stocky in build, and very proud of his long rusty sideburns. He had grey eyes and a wide grin, and he couldn't stop making funny remarks to save his life. You couldn't shut up that guy; he always had to get his two-bits' worth in. Hence his name. Even his teachers forgot his real name was Keith, and we hardly remembered he had one. Life was one big joke to Two-Bit.

1. Get into pairs. Go through this description of Two-Bit Matthews together. How much of it tells us what Two-Bit looked like?

   Why do you think the author chose these particular details about Two-Bit Matthews? What do they tell us about his personality? What part is he likely to play in the story?

2. Which parts of this description do you think are most interesting? What brings Two-Bit alive for you? What would your drawing of him be like?

Describing People

3 Imagine you are introducing a character into a story about people in your school.

Decide what kind of story the character is in. Jot down some ideas. Include a few details of his or her appearance.

Include at least one idea about how s/he behaves. Try to agree on what you think others find most noticeable about your person.

Write the description of this new character together and then try it out on another pair. See if it works.

4 A piece of description like the one you have been studying is a good way of getting to know a person. How can you find out what people are like in stories? Make a list of any other ways you can think of.

Separate descriptions of people or places do not happen very often in stories. Writers normally describe people and places together.

1 Read again the beginning of *The Eighteenth Emergency* on page 50. Does it describe people, places or both?

Can you think of anything else to add to your list of other ways of describing people now that you have read this again?

It is most important, when you are writing, to remember why you are doing it! For example, if you are trying to build up suspense, like Betsy Byars, you do not want to stop and have a long description of Benjie's front door or even of Benjie's mother. A good writer chooses when to use description and when to have people speaking or doing things.

Choosing the Right Moment

Deciding the right moment to include a description can be tricky. You need to be clear about what you are trying to do and how a new description will help your writing. This may depend on what kind of story you are writing. It may also depend on what point in your story you have reached.

1 Divide into small groups and study these four paragraphs. Each one is the beginning of a story or a chapter from a story written for young people of your age.

2 In pairs, see if you can match the paragraphs to their stories:

◆ an autobiography
◆ a horror story
◆ a story about animals
◆ a science fiction story

3 Look up any word you do not understand in a dictionary.

A

She walked up to the door and stopped. It was just an ordinary door, made of wood. It had been painted a shade of white once. Now it was so dirty it looked brown. But it was just an ordinary door. So why did she stand in front of it and tremble? She stretched out her hand towards the door handle. Her fingers touched the cold iron and drew back immediately as if they had been stung. What was that noise from behind the door? Was it someone laughing?

B

She walked up to the door and stopped. The sound of machinery humming rose suddenly. She wondered if the ship's atmosphere control system was finally going to pack up. She decided it was more likely that something the other side of the door was using energy to take decisions about her. To the right of the door a violet-coloured light flashed faintly. She had the clear impression that something was checking up on her. She had no choice now. She took out her identity card and slotted it carefully into the door's locking mechanism.

Choosing the Right Moment

C

She opened the door and then froze. Sitting on the kitchen table was the most enormous hedgehog. She did not know whether to cry out for help or to calm her fears and watch. It was drinking from her half-eaten cornflake bowl. For a moment it paused and looked at her. Moving clumsily in between the remains of their breakfast, it clambered towards her. Without a second thought she screamed and ran out of the door.

D

I ran out of the front door. Dad was shouting at me to slow down, but I took no notice. There was the normal crowd of school children waiting for the bus. I barged my way through them and out into the road at the front of the queue. With a terrible screeching of brakes, the taxi tried to slow down. There was a loud bang and my left leg buckled underneath me. I felt cold hard metal crushing me into the side of the bus.

4 In each of these paragraphs there is a door. Each writer had to decide how much time to spend describing the door. Which of them spend most space describing the door? Why is the door important to the story in each of these paragraphs?

5 Each one of these paragraphs tries to leave you guessing what will happen next. Choose one of them. On your own, continue the story by writing at least five more paragraphs.

Starting Writing

Decide who you are going to write your story for. What age group do you think each of the first paragraphs were written for? Choose a title for the story.
Plan out the events of your paragraphs. Make notes about what will happen or be described in each paragraph.

Composing

Continue the story in a rough draft, paying particular attention to your description. Make your paragraphs exciting, and try to choose the right moments for your descriptions.

Revising

Show your rough draft to someone else in your group. Talk to them about how you can improve your writing.
Make any changes in response to what you have heard.

Proof-reading

Check your spelling and punctuation.

Publishing

Produce your final copy.

The Describing Words

'Dogs nosed among crumpled paper in the gutter; a rusty bicycle-wheel lay on the cobbles.'

Many of the descriptions you have been reading came alive because of **adjectives** in them. An adjective is a word that tells you more about a noun.

In the sentence above, 'dogs', 'paper', 'gutter', 'bicycle-wheel' and 'cobbles' are nouns.

'crumpled' tells you more about the paper

'rusty' describes the bicycle-wheel

'Crumpled' and 'rusty' are adjectives. In these examples they come before the nouns they are telling you more about.

In your English lessons you will be learning about many different kinds of adjectives and the different places in which they can appear in a sentence.

1. Get into pairs. Why do you think the writer of the description of the alley bothered to tell us that the paper was crumpled and the bicycle-wheel was rusty?

2. Look again at the passages you have been studying. Make a list of all the words in two of them that seem to you to be adjectives.

3. For each adjective find the noun it goes with. What does each adjective tell you about its noun?

Adjectives All Around

You don't need to know what adjectives are to be able to use them! You use them yourself all the time. The more you realise how powerful they can be, the more you may choose to use them.

1. In pairs, describe

   your shoes, your partner, the room you are in, your house or flat, your road, a person you like, the place you like most.

2. Then have some fun by describing the same person in a completely different way, or an old but friendly shoe, or describe your house as if it were an ideal home.

The Describing Words

3 How often do your descriptions include adjectives? What would they be like if you removed all the adjectives? Try this by writing one of them down in full and then taking out the adjectives. What difference does it make? Together choose a new adjective for each noun. Write the new description down. Decide how your new description compares with your first. How are they different? Which one is better? Why?

4 In groups, look at these two pictures.

In what ways are they different? Make a list of all the changes.

Describe each change as exactly as you can, using the most suitable adjectives you can think of.

5 Listen to, and, if possible, tape record these things.

the weather forecast,
advertisements on the television,
a description of someone wanted for a robbery

How many of the words used in these examples are adjectives?

6 Make up your own description of yesterday's weather and write it down. Try and include a number of adjectives to bring it alive.

Perform your weather forecast as if you were on television. Video yourself.

You could use a thesaurus to help you choose some exciting new adjectives.

A thesaurus is a kind of dictionary, but instead of the meaning of words, a thesaurus gathers together words of similar meaning and shows you different ways of describing the same thing.

You could also present a weather forecast for some unusual weather, for example, for storms or floods.

When Did It Happen?

Look back to the cartoon of the caveman and cavewoman on page 35 of Unit 3, Making Words Work.

Sometimes you will want to describe things as they are actually happening, as in the first cartoon opposite. On many occasions you will prefer to describe them when they have finished happening, as in the second one.

In Unit 3, Making Words Work, you found out about words called verbs, like 'fall'. Verbs are interesting because they can have different **tenses**. Tenses tell you when something happened. If it is happening now, it is called the **present**. If it has happened before, it is called the **past**.

1 In pairs, decide which one of the two cartoons is set in the past and which in the present tense. The clue is in what they are saying.

Past or Present?

One of the choices a speaker or writer makes is whether to use the past or the present tense.

1 Study this commentary. It describes what happens in an ordinary garden at night.

Night in the Garden

At night the garden is quiet. There are no people about to laugh and talk. And the birds that have chirped and twittered in the branches all day are asleep in their roosts. But the moonlit garden is not empty. It only seems deserted because the creatures of the night are quieter than those of the day.

A mole toils steadily through the earth in its search for worms, leaving a tell-tale line of mole-hills across the lawn. A rat sniffs doubtfully at a large stag beetle to see if it would be good to eat. A hedgehog, ambling across a path, has no doubts about the slug it has found. A slug is what it has been looking for all evening.

Near the house, a fox startles itself and everybody else by knocking over a dustbin. It has learnt that there are sometimes tasty titbits inside. A hawkmoth rushes for safety as a bat swoops overhead. And from the garden seat, the domestic cat looks at the busy scene. It is as much a creature of the night as of the day, and is perfectly at home with the other animals of the night.

from *Animals at Night*, Christopher Tunney

2 In pairs, read this extract aloud.

Which of these statements do you think best describes it?

It seems to be a garden full of people.

It is like a television wildlife programme.

It seems to be described from a great distance.

It is hard to imagine what is being described.

It makes you feel as if you are there.

You can almost see and hear the animals in the garden.

Which tense do you think it is written in?

3 Now look at this.

At night the garden was quiet. There were no people about to laugh and talk. And the birds that had chirped and twittered in the branches all day were asleep in their roosts. But the moonlit garden was not empty ...

Which tense is this written in?

4 Does the way it is written now make it seem more or less vivid? Explain your reasons as clearly as you can.

This kind of passage is called a **commentary**. A commentary is intended to make you feel as if you are there, watching. Commentaries, whether they are about wildlife, sport or anything else, are normally written in the present tense.

1 In pairs, imagine you are either a sports commentator or doing the commentary for a television programme about rare animals.

2 Choose your sport or animal and practise together what you might say. Imagine you are watching the game or the animal and try to make what you say as exciting as possible for someone interested in the subject.

3 You have been asked by the television company to contribute to a book for young people to go with the sports or wildlife programme for which you are a commentator.

Stage 1
Tape record your commentary.

Stage 2
Carefully write down exactly what you have recorded.

Stage 3
Remove 'ers', 'ums', extra 'and's plus anything which makes it sound amateurish. You might find a wordprocessor particularly helpful at this stage.

Stage 4
Write it out as a short commentary similar to the one you read earlier on this page.

Responding to a Book

Throughout your English lessons you will be reading a number of novels. Sometimes you will want simply to read them. On other occasions you may wish to explore your reading by producing work based on what you have read. In the next section there are five suggestions of ways that you can respond to what you have read.

Five Things to Do with a Book

Study these alternatives. Some can be completed individually, some in pairs and some in small groups. You may find it helpful to come back to these pages when you are wanting to choose some follow-up work for yourself.

Keeping a reading log

A **reading log** is a special kind of diary. It is a record of all the thoughts and feelings you choose to jot down while you are reading a novel.

1 Look at this extract from a reading log. The book being read was *The Eighteenth Emergency* by Betsy Byars, the book referred to at the beginning of this Unit. During a period of two weeks the pupil made these notes and collected this newspaper article.

BOY FOUND AFTER RUNNING AWAY FROM HOME

Stephen Daniels, the twelve year old boy who ran away from home after school bullies threatened to beat him up, has turned up safe and well only a few miles from his home. He was found sleeping in a derelict building in the early hours of yesterday morning. According to police he was in good health but suffering from exhaustion.

Stephen's mother told reporters, "We are just happy to have him back. Now we want to get back to normal."

His head teacher said that Stephen was a sensitive boy who had taken the threats of some of the rougher elements in the school much too seriously. "We can assure Stephen and his family that there will be no intimidation of any kind when he returns to school."

Local M.P., Clive Kidderminster, has called for an inquiry into conditions in local schools. "This case may represent the tip of the ice-

---

The beginning is strange. Makes you read on to find out what is happening.

What are cracker jacks?

What is a day-bed?

Benjie's habit of writing notices is really weird (but funny)

Benjie's mum doesn't completely trust him.

Benjie and the dog fit together.

Benjie exaggerates.

Responding to a Book

2 Keep a reading log while you are reading a novel.

Decide how long you want to keep one. You could include your thoughts on

- how the novel begins
- how the story develops
- what you think about the characters and the way they act
- anything you find difficult
- how it ends
- anything it reminds you of, for example, other books or television programmes
- how it makes you feel, especially at the end

You could include any cuttings from newspapers or magazines that you think are at all similar to your story.

Remember – it is <u>your</u> reading log! Only show it to a friend or your teacher if you want to!

Making a tape recording

Stage 1

Choose the section of your novel that you enjoyed most.

Decide how many characters appear in your chosen section. Try not to choose one that has too many. If your book has a narrator, that is, someone who is in the story and who is telling it to the reader, you may want to count her or him in as well.

Stage 2

In a small group, decide who is going to read which character. You might decide to read one character each, or take more than one. Decide how each character would talk. (The person who has selected the section should have the final decision here!) Tape record your section.

Stage 3

Play it to other groups in the class. If you live near a hospital, you might like to see if your tape recording would be of interest to younger patients there.

Reading together

1 In a small group, choose one novel which each of you will read over a period of time. It is important that you all read the same novel for this activity.

Before you start reading the book, choose two points in the book (for example, when you reach a particular chapter) when you are all going to meet together as a group.

At these two moments, talk about

- what you are enjoying about the book
- what has happened so far and how you are reacting to the story
- which characters strike you as being particularly interesting
- what you think might happen next

2 When you have finished reading the book, prepare a presentation for the rest of your class. This should aim to give an idea of what the book is like and whether it might be of interest to them.

Include the following things.

- a reading of a key moment from the novel, that is, about one or two pages which you think are important and could be read out loud well.
- descriptions of a few of the characters. You could read out an example of how they speak.
- any useful information about the background to your story. For example, if you were talking about *The Eighteenth Emergency* at the start of this Unit, you might want to tell your listeners something about living in a city in the United States of America.
- a clear indication of whether you would recommend the book or not, and what age it is suitable for.

Responding to a Book

Illustrating a novel

You might like to do these activities with someone else.

Try some of these ideas for a novel you have read.

Design a new cover

1. Before you start, do some research by looking at other covers for books similar to the one you are designing for.

2. You could draw or paint an important scene from the book or one of the characters. You will need to decide what style of writing to use on the cover.

3. You might decide to have a completely different kind of cover.

Illustrate an important scene

1. Decide where it is set and what it looks like, using information from the book. Decide what any characters you include look like and what they would be wearing.

2. Choose one line from the novel to go with your artwork.

Draw a family tree

1. In many novels there is at least one family which you get to know closely. If this is the case, draw out a family tree for them showing the relationships between members of the family clearly. Maybe there is more than one family? Do their family tree as well.

Draw a map

1. Many novels contain journeys or are set in a particular area which you get to know well. Draw a map of any place described in detail or of any journey in your book. You could do this on your own.

In a group, you could make a large wall chart showing where characters were at various stages in the book. It could contain pictures of scenes and what characters said.

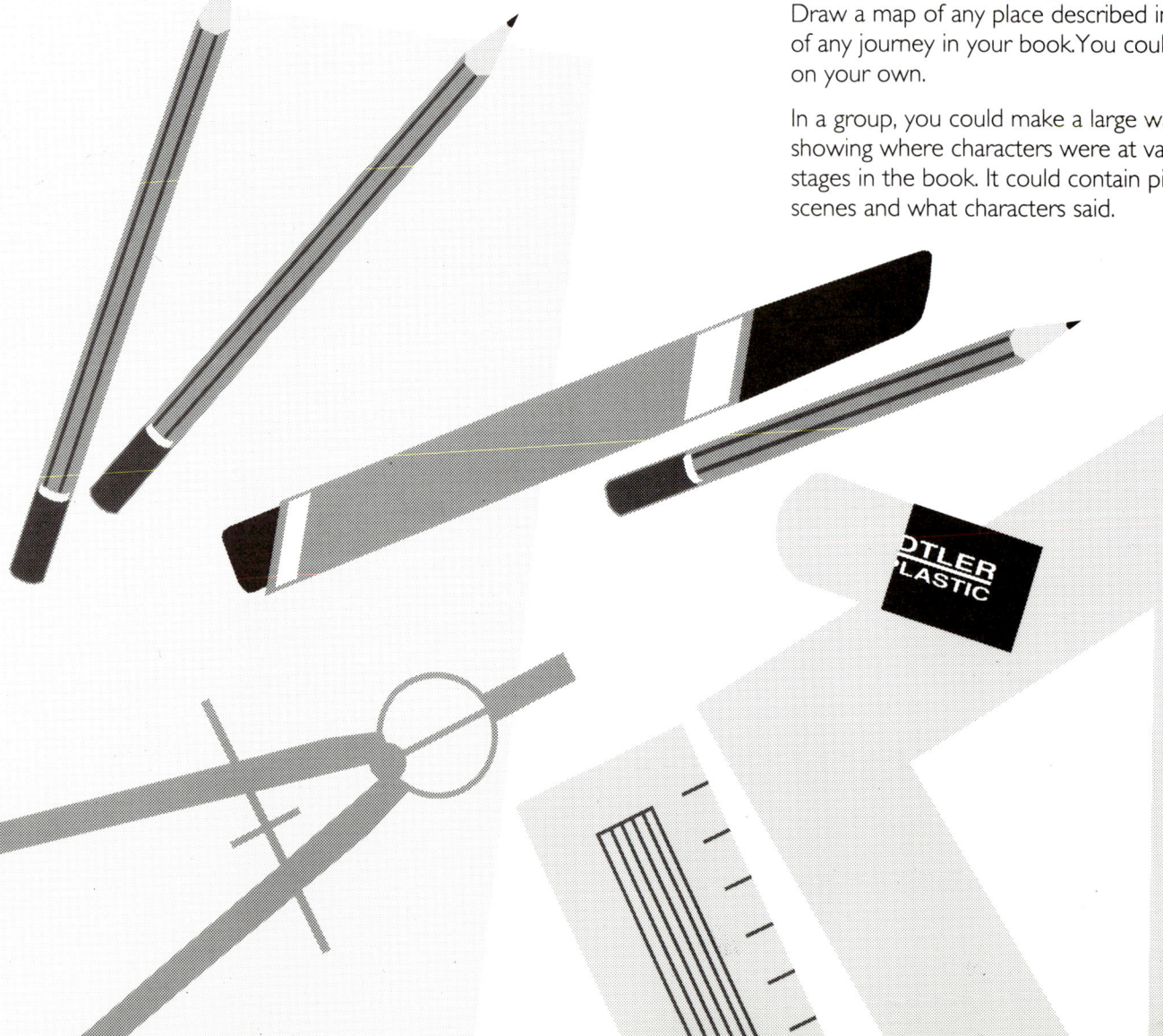

Responding to a Book

Questioning a book

1 In pairs, choose a chapter from one of the novels which you particularly enjoyed.

Make a list of fifteen questions that you can ask other members of the class. Make a note of your answers to them, too.

Try to choose questions which cannot be answered simply by yes or no and which encourage longer answers.

For example, if you were writing questions for the opening of *The Eighteenth Emergency* (at the start of this Unit), you might ask the following questions.

- ◆ As you read the first four paragraphs, why did you think the boy was running away?
- ◆ Which words from the opening make you think that the boy is very worried about something?
- ◆ Have you ever run away from something dangerous? If so, please explain how this happened and other details.

2 Put your questions on tape so that other members of the class can listen to them and discuss their answers with you.

3 Your class could prepare a series of tapes with questions about different novels. You could make a pack to go with the tape. It could include a copy of the chapter and some possible answers (with your names marked next to them) to your questions.

You could put these in an envelope so that they would only be used when the listener had tried his or her best to answer them!

Reflection

In this Unit you have been practising how to

- *express opinions in a group discussion*
- *use a tape recorder in a small group presentation*
- *make a list of relevant questions to ask about a book you have read*
- *recognise and write simple paragraphs*
- *talk about descriptions in stories*
- *produce descriptions for a purpose*
- *record your opinions about what you are reading*

Talk to your friends and your teacher about the things you have been doing in this Unit. Decide how much you have understood and how much progress you have made. Filling in Unit 5 of the Record Sheet on page 76 will also help you think about what you have done in this Unit and the knowledge you are gaining in your English lessons.

65

Unit 6 Getting to Grips with Language

This Unit gives you the opportunity to
- *recognise that sentences have subjects*
- *respond to instructions*
- *re-tell a story in your own words*
- *use a variety of connecting words*
- *find out more about how language began*

1. As part of a small group, study these groups of words. Each of them has something to do with the holiday scene below.

   sitting in the sun

   playing on the beach

   kicked the ball

   The beach was very crowded

   kicked sand in her face

   Rachel kicked the football

   She went swimming in the sea

   very crowded

   sea blue

   The sea was cold

2. Which of these groups of words make complete sense to you as you read them along each line? Make a list of the groups that do.

   For example

   kicked the ball

   nearly makes sense, but doesn't make complete sense because you do not know **who** kicked it.

   A sentence must make complete sense. You should be able to read one and feel that nothing has been left out. To do this it needs to have a **subject**. A subject is a kind of noun. It is the name given to a noun which you are being told something about.

   For example

   Rachel kicked the football.

   Rachel is the name of a person.
   Rachel is a noun.
   Rachel is the subject of the sentence.
   With Rachel in it, the sentence makes complete sense.

What is a Subject?

Like a lot of things in language, it isn't easy to be absolutely exact about what a subject is. You might say that in the example above you are being told something about the football as well as about Rachel. That is true. But the difference is this.

Sentence Rule No. 3 The subject of a sentence controls the verb.

(If you cannot remember what a verb is, look back to Unit 3, Making Words Work, on page 36.)

Sometimes the subject of a sentence is a word like he, she, it, we, you or they. These words are a special kind of noun called **pronouns**.

1 In pairs, study these sentences. In each one decide which word is the subject.

The beach was very crowded.

She went swimming in the sea.

The sea was cold.

It was freezing.

Beach-football is great fun.

Sand keeps getting in my sandwiches.

The donkey is standing on my foot.

2 Look at the picture. Imagine it is one of your holiday snaps and that you are describing it to a friend. Taking it in turns, make up sentences about the picture. Try and make them as interesting or amusing as possible. After each sentence decide what the subject of the sentence you have just made up is.

You will be learning more about sentences later in your English lessons. For now it will help you to write in sentences if you remember

Sentence Rule No. 4 To make complete sense a sentence must have a subject.

The Sentences Game

In this story you are going to be the subject of many of the sentences. The tale can be told in many different ways, depending on the order of your choice.

In pairs, work out your own version of the story. This is done by taking it in turns to read out each alternative as you come to it. Start at number **1**. Make a note in particular of the numbers you move in the order you choose them to make your own version of the story.

Rescue the hostage from the palace of the evil king.

1 You are standing in a courtyard. Roads lead north or south. Which way do you go?

   north – Go to 2

   south – Go to 24

2 You see a lever in the wall beside you. You can pull it to the left or the right. Which do you choose?

   left – Go to 4

   right – Go to 3

3 A hidden door opens. You find yourself in the royal bedroom. You can hear voices in the corridor outside. You must hide. Do you choose under the bed or behind the curtains?

   under the bed – Go to 5

   behind the curtains – Go to 15

4 A hidden door opens. You find yourself in the palace kitchen. A servant is just leaving the room with a tray of drinks. You pick up a tray and follow him. Does he speak to you?

   yes – Go to 11

   no – Go to 10

5 You are seen and killed. Your quest has failed.

6 You overhear servants saying that the hostage is kept in the storeroom with the blue door. Do you try to force them to take you there or do you wait and think?

   force them to take you there – Go to 13

   wait and think – Go to 22

7 The king mentions that the hostage is kept in the storeroom with the blue door. You make an excuse and leave. Just outside the bathroom a dagger is fixed to the wall. Do you take it down?

   yes – Go to 14

   no – Go to 9

The Sentences Game

8 Two tunnels open in front of you. Do you take (a) or (b)?

(a) – Go to 15

(b) – Go to 17

9 Guards see you and attack. You have no weapon and are killed instantly. Your quest has failed.

10 The servant was really a robber. Armed guards come running down the corridor. They seize you both and throw you into a dungeon. Your quest has failed.

11 The servant tells you that the hostage is kept in the storeroom with the blue door. You make your way there. The door is locked. Do you break it down or do you knock and call out the hostage's name?

break the door down – Go to 20

call out the hostage's name – Go to 24

12 You find yourself in the royal bathroom. The king is having a bath. Do you hand him a towel or try to take him hostage?

hand him a towel – Go to 7

take him hostage – Go to 21

13 Guards come running down the corridor. You are seized and thrown into a dungeon. Your quest has failed.

14 The dagger was really an alarm. Guards come running. Do you run or stay and fight?

run – Go to 19

fight – Go to 8

15 You are on a landing. Stairs lead up and down. Which way do you go?

up – Go to 16

down – Go to 12

16 You see a beggar limping along the corridor. Do you follow him?

yes – Go to 4

no – Go to 17

17 You find yourself in the palace guardroom. Armour is hanging on the wall. Do you put it on to disguise yourself or not?

yes – Go to 6

no – Go to 9

The Sentences Game

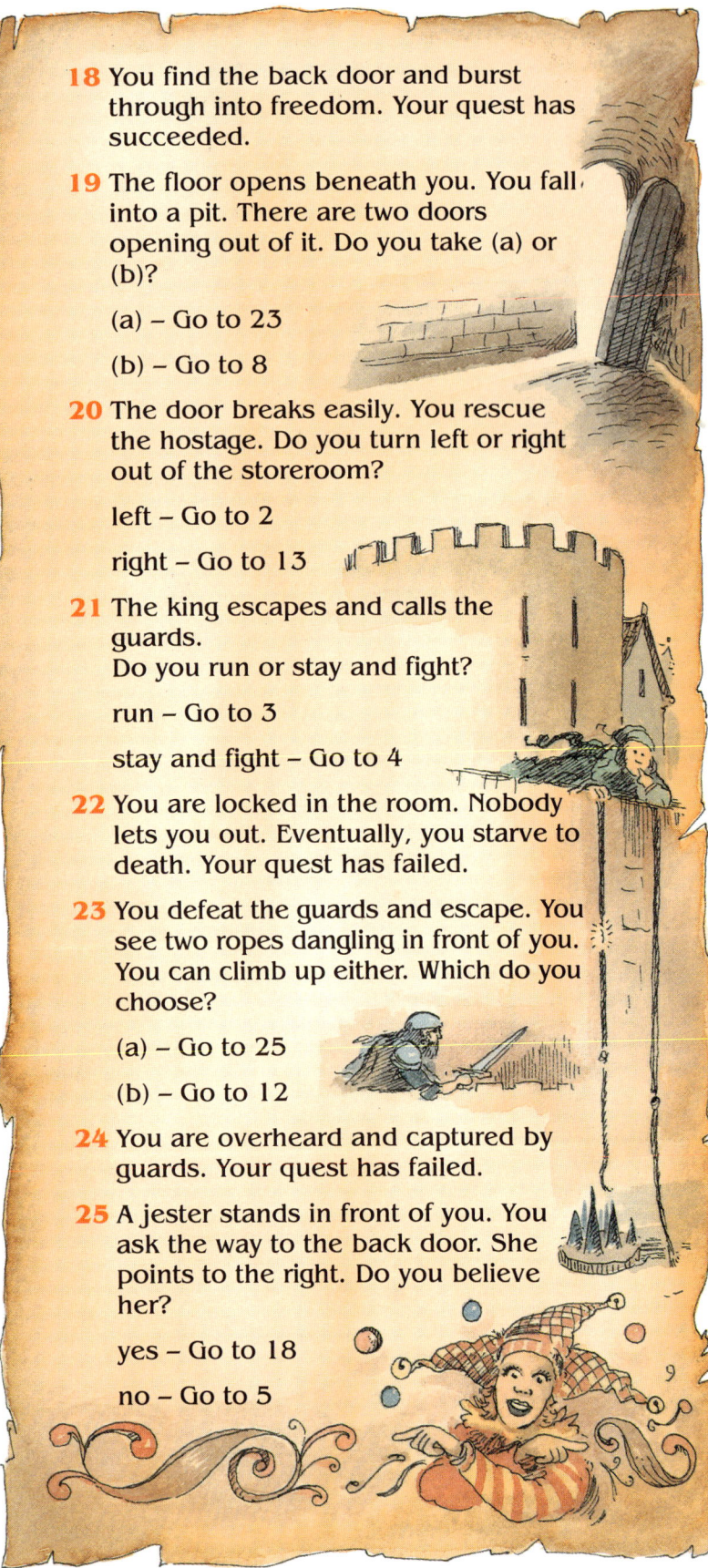

18 You find the back door and burst through into freedom. Your quest has succeeded.

19 The floor opens beneath you. You fall into a pit. There are two doors opening out of it. Do you take (a) or (b)?

(a) – Go to 23

(b) – Go to 8

20 The door breaks easily. You rescue the hostage. Do you turn left or right out of the storeroom?

left – Go to 2

right – Go to 13

21 The king escapes and calls the guards.
Do you run or stay and fight?

run – Go to 3

stay and fight – Go to 4

22 You are locked in the room. Nobody lets you out. Eventually, you starve to death. Your quest has failed.

23 You defeat the guards and escape. You see two ropes dangling in front of you. You can climb up either. Which do you choose?

(a) – Go to 25

(b) – Go to 12

24 You are overheard and captured by guards. Your quest has failed.

25 A jester stands in front of you. You ask the way to the back door. She points to the right. Do you believe her?

yes – Go to 18

no – Go to 5

1 Choose four numbers from your story in the order you wrote them down. As an example, say you had moved in the order 1 2 4 11.

2 Describe your story to your partner by moving from step to step. It might sound like this:

I was standing in a courtyard. There were two roads leading from it. I decided to head north. **At that moment** I noticed a lever on the wall beside me. I pulled it to the left. A hidden door opened.

I found myself in the palace kitchen. A servant was just leaving the room with a tray of drinks.

Then I had a thought. I picked up a tray and followed him. **Unfortunately** the servant turned round and started to talk to me ...

3 Listen to your partner's version carefully. How many times did s/he use the word **then**? Did s/he start sentences with **And** or **And then**? If so, do you think these words make the story sound more interesting or not?

4 Look at the example above again. In it three different ways of connecting sentences are used; these are in the heavier print.

There are a variety of different words that can be used at the start of a new sentence to connect it with the one before.

Here are some examples of possible connecting words that you could use in a story like this.

Suddenly

Next

Soon

Later

After

Unfortunately

Then

1 How many more can you think of? Make a list of them.

The Sentences Game

2 Study your version of the story again. Tell it to your partner trying to use as many different ways of connecting your sentences together as you can.

3 On your own, write your own version of The Sentences Game, following these steps.

Stage 1

Using your chosen set of numbers, produce a rough draft of your story.

Stage 2

Test it out on your partner, using a good variety of connecting words.

Stage 3

Produce a final draft. If you can, either write it in old-fashioned handwriting or illustrate it.

You might like to make a tape recording of your story using your own sound effects.

Have you read any other branching stories like this which allow you to choose your own plot? You might like to bring them into class to share.

Writing your own branching story is fun but not easy. This one had to be planned out very carefully first, using a diagram like this. Copy the diagram and add boxes to it to see how the story fits together. To plan the whole story you need a very big piece of paper!

Now try one of your own. Keep it very simple to start with. Get a friend to check that it works.

Language and Thought

Pictures were probably the earliest kind of language. For example, there are very old drawings on caves in many parts of the world.

Talking without Words

1. In small groups, find out some information about early cave paintings. Copy some of the pictures that you find. What do they mostly show?

2. We still use pictures instead of words today to communicate certain kinds of information. These are normally called **pictograms**. Pictograms give us a message using a picture. Pictograms are often used in signs. In your groups, study these common examples. Decide what you think each one means.

 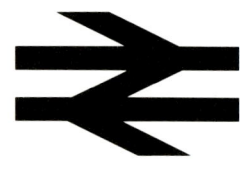 

3. How many of these do you know? Write them down with an explanation next to them. Say what they are and what they mean.

4. In pairs, make up your own pictograms for

   traffic-jam

   snow on the road

   Silence

   airport

   No Fishing

   Danger

5. Make up a set of pictograms to describe the way people might feel in your school, such as happy, miserable, cheeky. Include some for teachers and parents as well as students.

6. Why do you think pictograms are used all round the world? Can you make up some rules for drawing successful pictograms?

No-one knows exactly when or how speech began or exactly when men and women began to write down what they said.

It was fairly easy to draw pictures of most objects and animals. It must have been far more difficult to draw ideas and feelings. Throughout the world various languages developed so that people could communicate their ideas to each other. These languages are still developing and changing all the time.

Today we use language in four linked ways:

speaking   listening   writing   reading

The more we use language and think about how we are using it, the more we know and understand how we speak, listen, write and read.

Language and Thought

1. In groups, discuss which one of these ways of using language you think you use most now. Does it vary depending on which lesson you are studying or what activity you are involved in? Does it depend on whether you are in or out of school? Which one do you think takes most effort?

   How do you think early women and men developed what we call language? In which order do you think they learnt to speak, listen, write and read?

Developing an Alphabet

It is generally agreed that the first alphabet was invented by the Phoenicians who lived on the eastern side of the Mediterranean. Later the Greeks began to trade with them and based their alphabet on what they saw. It looked like this.

How many of these letters do you recognise as part of the English language. Why do you think this is?

We get the name alphabet from the first two Greek letters,

Alpha   Beta

ΑΒΓΔΕΙΗΘΙΚΛΜΝΞΟΓΡϹΤΥΦΧΨΩ

абвгдежзийклмнопрстуфх

אבגדהוזחטיכלמנסעפצקרשתתסזףץ

آأتبثتثنيثتثـجخـجذزرشـشـششض

As you know, some people are **bilingual**, that is they can speak in two different languages. Is there anyone who can do this in your class? To speak and understand more than one language is a special ability.

1. In groups or as a class, see how many of the above alphabets you recognise. Your bilingual friends may be able to help you.

   There are many different alphabets and languages in use in the world today. For example, more than 150 languages are used in London schools.

2. Using the knowledge in your class or the library and any other reference source you can think of, find as many examples of different alphabets as you can.

   Find out which languages are spoken by the largest number of people throughout the world. Decide on a way of presenting this information to other groups in your class.

73

Making Up a New Language

Many writers enjoy making up new words.

1. How much of this famous poem can you understand?

   Many of these words were completely made up by Lewis Carroll. You can guess what some of them mean by putting words that you know together, for example, **mimsy** is made up of **miserable** and **flimsy**.

2. In pairs, read the poem aloud several times. Listen carefully to it. What do you think the poem sounds as if it is about?

3. Make a list of all the words you do not recognise. Try looking them up in the dictionary. See if they remind you of any other words. Guess the meaning of each of these words.

4. Try to tell the story of this poem to each other.

5. Why do you think that Lewis Carroll chose to make up words for a poem about a Jabberwocky? Think of as many reasons as you can and talk about them.

6. In pairs, write a poem of your own about an imaginary creature. Make it suitable for reading in your class.

Jabberwocky

'Twas brillig and the slithy toves
Did gyre and gimble in the wabe;
All mimsy were the borogroves,
And the mome raths outgrabe.

'Beware the Jabberwock, my son!
The jaws that bite, the claws that catch!
Beware the jubjub bird, and shun
The frumious Bandersnatch!'

He took his vorpal sword in hand:
Long time the manxone foe he sought
So rested he by the tumtum tree,
And stood awhile in thought.

And as in uffish thought he stood,
The Jabberwock with eyes of flame,
Came whittling through the tulgey wood,
And burbled as it came!

One, two! One, two! And through and through
The vorpal blade went snicker-snack!
He left it dead, and with its head
He went galumphing back.

'And hast thou slain the Jabberwock?
Come to my arms, my beamish boy!
O frabjous day! Callooh! Callay!'
He chortled in his joy.

'Twas brillig and the slithy toves
Did gyre and gimble in the wabe;
All mimsy were the borogroves,
And the mome raths outgrabe.

Lewis Carroll

Making Up a New Language

Starting Writing

Think of a new word for your creature.

Make up a number of new words to use in your poem about the creature, paying particular attention to their sound.

Decide what is going to happen in your poem.

Composing

Produce a rough draft. You could use the same pattern as *Jabberwocky* and have four lines to a verse.

Revising

Read it to your partner. Get their comments and make notes on any changes you want.

Proof-reading

Check your spelling and punctuation.

Publishing

Write out your final draft.

You might like to perform your poem to the class or record it.

Reflection

In this Unit you have been practising how to

- *follow instructions*
- *tell a story orally, that is, using the spoken word*
- *read a story aloud*
- *use a variety of connecting words to shape a story*
- *read, understand and use pictograms*
- *write a poem about an imaginary creature*

Talk to your friends and your teacher about the things you have been doing in this Unit. Decide how much you have understood and how much progress you have made. Filling in Unit 6 of the Record Sheet on page 76 will also help you think about what you have done in this Unit and the knowledge you are gaining in your English lessons.

Record Sheet for Units 4, 5 and 6

Important: Your teacher will give you photocopied versions of these two pages so that you do not need to write in this book.

First of all, with a friend, talk about and decide what the short statements mean. Discuss what you have been practising in English and how much you have understood of what you have done.

Next to each statement there are three targets to aim for. This is what they mean:

I understand this and have practised it.

I have done this with help.

I feel able to do this again.

If you are not sure what a statement means or whether you can do what it says, discuss it with your teacher.

Put a tick under the target that you think best describes what you can do. If you are in doubt, please ask for help.

Name of Student

I can

Unit 4
- take part in a group presentation
- express opinions clearly
- use information books and equipment in the school library
- make a list of questions to help select a reference book
- predict events in a story
- talk about setting and characters in a story
- show understanding that stories have a beginning, middle and end
- write a story with a clear beginning, middle and end
- use a dictionary to check for spelling
- discuss the organisation of writing while drafting it

Unit 5
- express opinions in a group discussion
- use a tape recorder in a small group presentation
- make a list of relevant questions to ask about a book I have read
- recognise and write simple paragraphs
- talk about descriptions in stories
- produce descriptions for a purpose
- record my opinions about what I am reading

Unit 6
- follow instructions
- tell a story orally
- read a story aloud
- use a variety of connecting words to shape a story
- read, understand and use pictograms
- write a poem about an imaginary creature

Record of Achievement in English

			Other Comments

Thinking Back

◆ Which is the best piece of work that you have done so far? Why do you think it was particularly successful?

◆ Which of the activities in the last three Units did you enjoy most?

◆ What have you learned about language that you did not know before?

◆ Was there anything you did not understand and would like more help with?

Thinking Forward

◆ Where do you think you need to improve most? What can you do to help you do so?

◆ What kind of activities can you suggest to your teacher that you could do as extra work?

Unit 7 Thinking About the Future

This Unit gives you the opportunity to

- *perform a play*
- *set out a play script*
- *use the exclamation mark*
- *explain your opinions*
- *play a role*
- *use the future tense*

1 Read this play in groups of five.

Survival of the Fittest

Characters
The Computer

Lloyd

Aisha

Siobhan

Rob

Scene 1
The command room of a spaceship. Four young people are sitting, facing a computer.

COMPUTER: Can I have everyone's attention please? Thank you. All right, now you've seen the printout, so you all know the position. Our mission cannot succeed in its present form.

LLOYD: (*In a shocked voice*) But it has to succeed!

Play for Tomorrow

AISHA:	Surely there must be some solution?
COMPUTER:	That is what I have called you all here to discuss. I have run the calculations through the Critical Situation Program. It is designed for use in only an absolute emergency.
LLOYD:	How does it work?
COMPUTER:	It considers all possible alternative solutions, no matter how remote.
SIOBHAN:	And what did it come up with?
COMPUTER:	Have any of you ever heard the expression 'survival of the fittest'?
SIOBHAN:	(*Uncertainly*) I think I have.
COMPUTER:	And do you know what it means?
SIOBHAN:	I think so. It's how nature works. Animals and humans. The weak ones die out. That way the species as a whole keeps strong and survives.
COMPUTER:	Exactly.
LLOYD:	What has that got to do with anything?
COMPUTER:	Be patient, Lloyd. Now I wonder which one of the crew is the weakest?
ROB:	(*Grinning stupidly*) It's bound to be one of the girls.
SIOBHAN:	Oh yeah? Want to try out your theory, Muscles?

Play for Tomorrow

COMPUTER: Just a minute. It's not that simple. Strength or weakness aren't just measured in simple physical terms.

ROB: What do you mean?

SIOBHAN: He means that brains come into it as well.

ROB: Which also counts you out.

SIOBHAN: (*Getting up and walking away angrily*) God, you're so childish.

AISHA: Could you two please stop quarrelling for once? This is important. Please go on, Computer.

COMPUTER: As Siobhan has correctly observed, there are many qualities which go to make up a human being. They are not all obvious. Each one of you has many hidden strengths.

SIOBHAN: (*Returning to her seat*) And weaknesses, in Rob's case.

ROB: Such as?

COMPUTER: Such as leadership, courage, experience ...

ROB: That's me you're describing.

COMPUTER: Imagination, intuition, patience.

SIOBHAN: What does intuition mean?

Play for Tomorrow

AISHA: It means trusting to your instinct, knowing how you feel about something.

COMPUTER: The list of human qualities is enormous. I'm sure you can think for yourself what you value in another person.

LLOYD: But where is all this getting us?

AISHA: And what's it got to do with the survival of the fittest?

COMPUTER: The nearest oxygen-bearing planet is a million light years from here.

LLOYD: We know that.

COMPUTER: This spaceship will only suppport three people for that distance. There are four of you.

SIOBHAN: We know that as well. We thought you'd got some sort of a solution to offer, Computer.

LLOYD: I think it has.

AISHA: What do you mean?

LLOYD: I think it's telling us that one crew member will have to go. Am I right, Computer?

COMPUTER: To put it bluntly, yes.

SIOBHAN: Go where?

Rob: Through the airlock, dumb-dumb.

Aisha: (*Shouting*) But that's inhuman!

Rob: Naturally, it was thought up by a computer.

Aisha: I'm not having anything to do with it.

Computer: Your first duty is to the survival of the human race, Aisha. That was why we were sent from Earth – to be the seeds of a new race.

Aisha: But isn't this what destroyed the Earth in the first place, people refusing to share resources?

Computer: It was much more complicated than that. Anyway there's no comparison. They had enough to go around. You don't.

Aisha: I'm still not doing it.

Computer: You don't have a choice. The Critical Situation Program has already been activated. You will not be able to leave these seats. Anyone who refuses to take part will automatically be ejected from the ship.

Lloyd: What if we all refuse?

Computer: I don't think you will. Rob?

Rob: It's better that one of us should be ejected now than that we should all die slowly.

Aisha: I'm not sure it is.

Computer: It's a matter of survival.

Aisha: Yes, but survival as what?

Rob: What do you mean?

Lloyd: She means that the rest of us may survive but will we be able to call ourselves human afterwards?

COMPUTER: No one need feel that he or she is personally to blame. You only have to key in the name of the person you think least fit to survive. That person will automatically be ejected.

ROB: After all there's no sense in us all dying together.

AISHA: (*Horrified*) I don't know how you can say that!

SIOBHAN: I think he's got a point.

AISHA: Lloyd, you're not going to go along with this, surely?

COMPUTER: Aisha, this is a necessary procedure. Now please, no more delays. Make your choice.

LLOYD: But how are we supposed to decide who ought to go?

COMPUTER: You must use your judgement. You each have an important job on this ship. Lloyd as Medical Officer is responsible for the health of the whole crew. Siobhan as Weapons Officer is responsible for dealing with any conflict that might arise. Aisha as Leisure Officer is responsible for the psychological well-being and happiness of you all. Rob, as Communications Officer, is responsible for making contact with any other life forms that you encounter. None of you can really be spared. But one of you must go. I shall allow you a short space of time to each make a case for your own preservation.

2 This activity is a **role-play** exercise. Role-play means imagining what someone else would do or say in a situation you have been given. You pretend to be them.

Take the part of one of the four characters, Lloyd, Aisha, Siobhan or Rob, and someone play the part of The Computer. You are going to try to convince the other members of your group that you should not be ejected from the ship. The person playing the part of The Computer will judge whose case is best.

Follow these steps.

Stage 1

Think hard about your position and why you should not be ejected. Make notes. Prepare a speech, stating what is so essential about your job.

Stage 2

Try your speech out on the other characters. Improvise a scene in which you each try to persuade the others that you should not be ejected.

Stage 3

While each of the arguments is being heard, the person playing The Computer should take brief notes on the main points made. At the end, she or he can decide to eject any one of the four crew members!

Stage 4

Now read the ending that the author decided on. How does yours compare?

Play for Tomorrow

Scene 2

The same spaceship command room, a short time after.

COMPUTER: Well, crew members, you have had enough time for discussion. You must now choose.

AISHA: This is horrible!

COMPUTER: In front of you are four buttons. The screen will indicate which button to push for which person. Will you please push your buttons now. (*Pause*) You have chosen Aisha.

AISHA: No – wait. You can't do this to me!

COMPUTER: Goodbye, Aisha.

ROB: Oh well, that's over and done with.

SIOBHAN: God, you're a monster, you are.

ROB: You're the Weapons Officer. I thought killing didn't bother you.

SIOBHAN: I never said that. I've got a job to do and I do it.

LLOYD: She was the nicest one of us.

ROB: But it was a matter of survival.

SIOBHAN: Survival of the fittest.

COMPUTER: Attention! Attention! Alien spacecraft approaching at unbelievable speed.

LLOYD: Where does it come from?

COMPUTER: I do not recognise it. My sensors reveal that the crew are humanoid and oxygen-breathing.

LLOYD: Oxygen-breathing! We're in luck!

COMPUTER: But radio messages emanating from the ship are not in any of the seven million languages which I can identify.

SIOBHAN:	Looks like this one's for you, Rob. Now let's see how useful you really are.
ROB:	Shut up, I'm working on this message. In the meantime, hadn't you better put the weapons system on alert?
SIOBHAN:	I already have, dumb-dumb. Now what are they saying?
ROB:	I don't know. Give me a chance.
SIOBHAN:	Shall I fire a warning shot?
LLOYD:	No! Don't do that. They might be able to help us.
SIOBHAN:	They might kill us.
LLOYD:	We've got to find out what they're saying.
ROB:	It's coming, it's coming.
COMPUTER:	Attention! Attention! The aliens have stopped their ship.
SIOBHAN:	What are they doing?
COMPUTER:	They are picking up Aisha and taking her on board.
SIOBHAN:	Is she still alive?
LLOYD:	Of course she is. There was plenty of air in her suit.
SIOBHAN:	Maybe they'll rescue us all. Have you worked out that message yet?
ROB:	Nearly.
COMPUTER:	Warning! The aliens are going away again.
SIOBHAN:	They mustn't do that. We need their help.
COMPUTER:	They are moving at incredible speed. They will be out of radio range in a few seconds.
LLOYD:	We've got to speak to them. Rob, for God's sake what did their message say?
ROB:	I've got it. (*Reading*) "Greetings earth people. We of the planet Noslen have been searching space for centuries, seeking an answer to the terrible sickness which besets our planet, the great Boredom. For so long now our people have wasted away, hopelessly searching for something new to do. We had almost given up hope when we encountered your ship. A brainscan of the crew showed us that your Leisure Officer had the answer to our problems. Locked in her mind are the rules of dozens of games completely unknown on our planet. We therefore re-programmed your computer with the Critical Situation Program, a little invention of ours. We knew we could rely on you to do the rest for us. We are returning now to our own world. We would like you to know that we have not had so much fun for several million years. So long suckers. P.S. Aisha sends her love."

Play for Tomorrow

3 How different was your ending from this one?

Why do you think the crew chose Aisha?

Why do you think the author chose to end the play like this?

There are four main ways of finding out about characters in plays.

◆ by listening to what they say
For example, you might decide that Rob is a sensible, reasonable person because of his point on page 82 that it is better that one of them dies.

◆ by looking at what they do
You might think that Siobhan is impatient because of the way that she gets up from her chair on page 80.

◆ by thinking about what the author says about them
Rob may seem childish and with a stupid view of the differences between men and women because the author describes him 'grinning stupidly' on page 79

◆ by thinking about what the other characters say about them
Rob might seem childish because of what Siobhan says about him on page 80 ('God, you're so childish.')

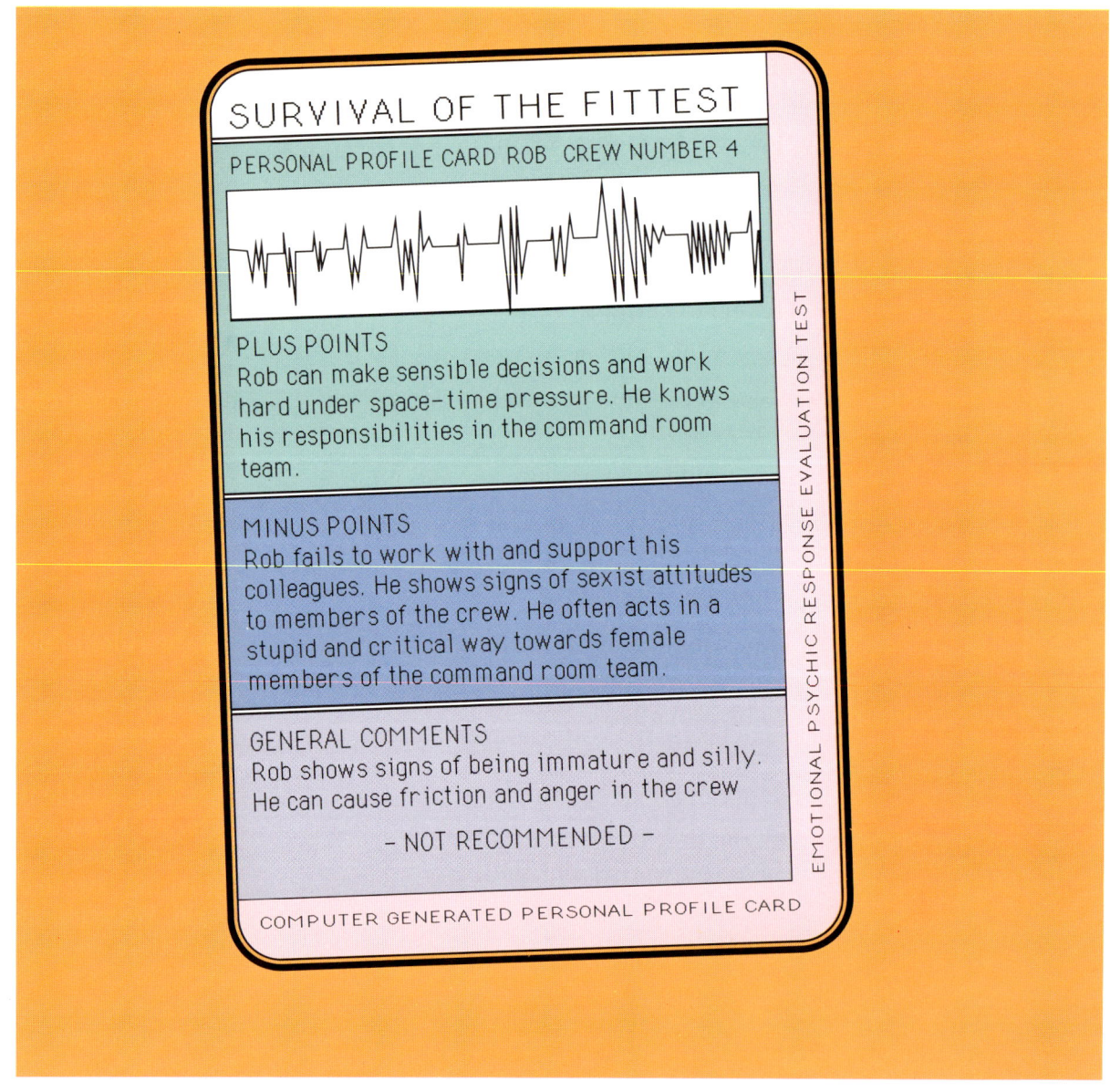

Play for Tomorrow

1. In your groups, go through the play again. Pick out clues like the ones above to help you decide what you think each of the characters is like. Make brief notes. You may wish to use the notes made by the person playing The Computer earlier on.

2. Prepare a personal profile on each character, including their positive and negative points. Give examples of each person's behaviour.

   Make your own profile cards for your group based on the one opposite and fill in the details.

3. Imagine you are a fifth human being on this ship. What might your job be?

   What are your own plus points? What are your negative ones? For example, are you sympathetic, bad-tempered, helpful, etc.

4. Fill in a personal profile for yourself.

   This is best done in pairs. Show your personal profile to your partner. When you are looking at your partner's profile, comment on what you see, and ask your partner to demonstrate the qualities listed on it, by giving you examples of the things she or he has done as evidence.

Using the Exclamation Mark

1. Read this short extract from the play.

   COMPUTER: Attention! Attention! Alien spacecraft approaching at unbelievable speed.

   LLOYD: Where does it come from?

   COMPUTER: I do not recognise it. My sensors reveal that the crew are humanoid and oxygen-breathing.

   LLOYD: Oxygen-breathing! We're in luck!

   At various points in the play there are **exclamation marks**. An exclamation mark (!) makes a sentence stronger. It is used when someone says something urgent or loud or surprising. For example, in the passage above, Lloyd is surprised to hear that the people on the ship are oxygen-breathing. He is also probably shouting.

2. Choose one part of *Survival of the Fittest*. Find the sentences which end with an exclamation mark. Read these out aloud. Decide why an exclamation mark has been used.

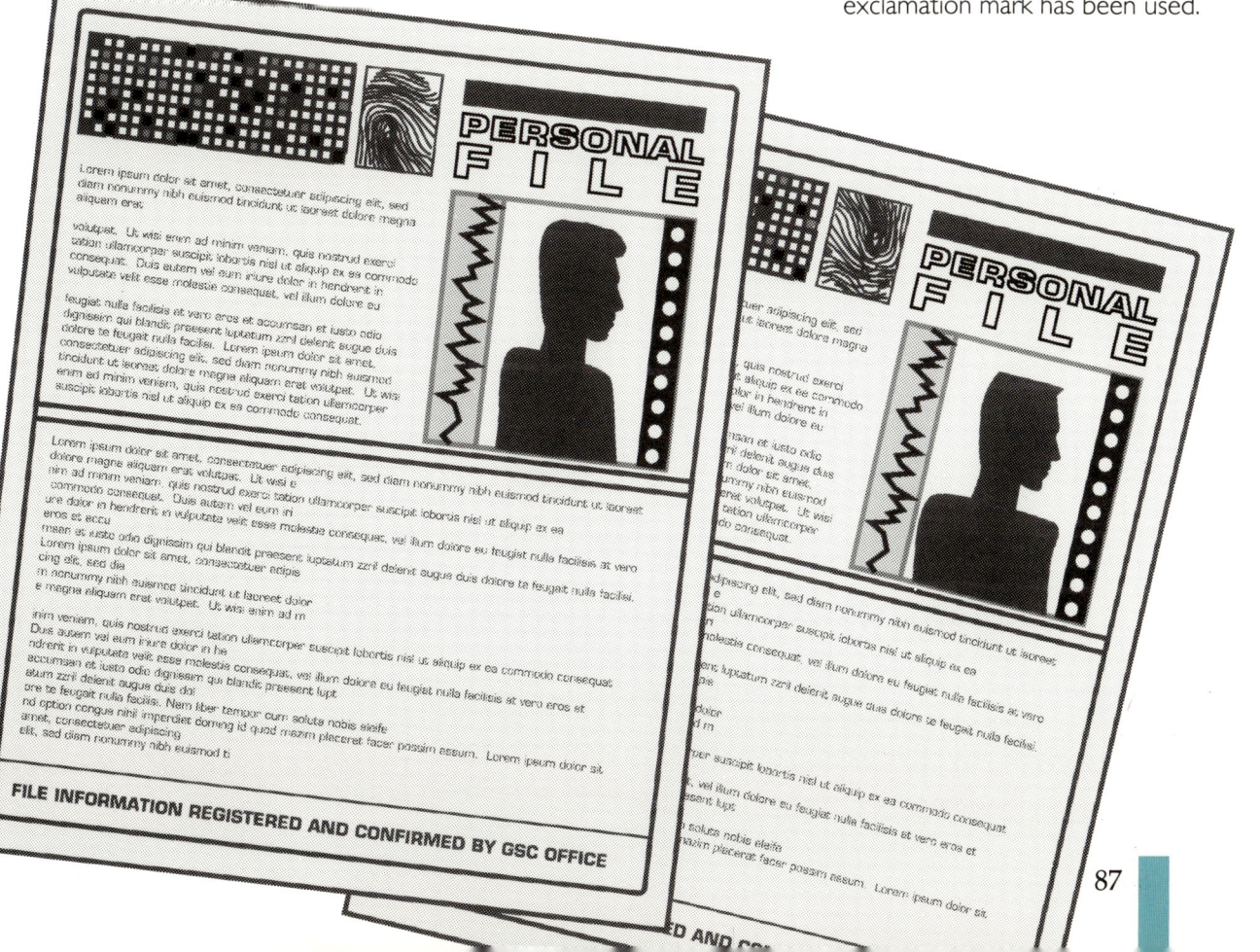

Setting Out a Script

A play script is set out in a special way. It has to contain the speech (what the characters say) and the information needed to help the actors read and act out the play.

Look back at page 84 in *Survival of the Fittest*. This is the dramatic moment when Aisha is thrown off the spacecraft.

1 In pairs, talk about the best way this action could be carried out in the play. Decide on a way and write the stage direction that gets Aisha out of the scene.

2 Here is a diagram. Look carefully at it. It shows the opening of the play. The important things to remember are pointed out for you.

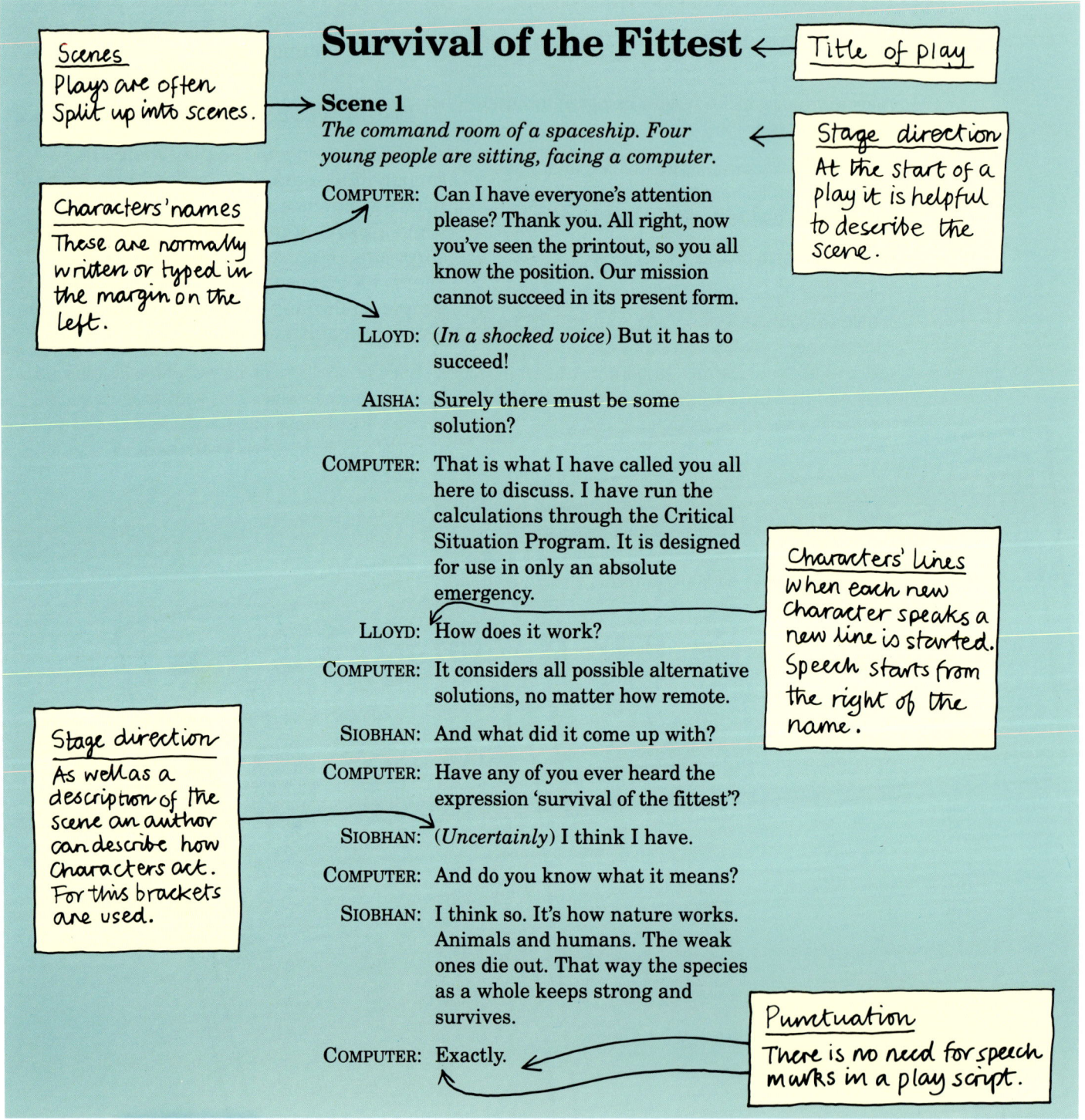

Title of play: Survival of the Fittest

Scenes: Plays are often split up into scenes. → Scene 1

Stage direction: At the start of a play it is helpful to describe the scene. — *The command room of a spaceship. Four young people are sitting, facing a computer.*

Characters' names: These are normally written or typed in the margin on the left.

COMPUTER: Can I have everyone's attention please? Thank you. All right, now you've seen the printout, so you all know the position. Our mission cannot succeed in its present form.

LLOYD: (*In a shocked voice*) But it has to succeed!

AISHA: Surely there must be some solution?

COMPUTER: That is what I have called you all here to discuss. I have run the calculations through the Critical Situation Program. It is designed for use in only an absolute emergency.

LLOYD: How does it work?

COMPUTER: It considers all possible alternative solutions, no matter how remote.

SIOBHAN: And what did it come up with?

COMPUTER: Have any of you ever heard the expression 'survival of the fittest'?

SIOBHAN: (*Uncertainly*) I think I have.

COMPUTER: And do you know what it means?

SIOBHAN: I think so. It's how nature works. Animals and humans. The weak ones die out. That way the species as a whole keeps strong and survives.

COMPUTER: Exactly.

Characters' lines: When each new character speaks a new line is started. Speech starts from the right of the name.

Stage direction: As well as a description of the scene an author can describe how characters act. For this brackets are used.

Punctuation: There is no need for speech marks in a play script.

Setting Out a Script

3 Study this story.

Stage 1

In pairs, decide what is happening in the story, and then what each of the characters is saying. Write it down as you decide what is in the blank speech bubbles.

Stage 2

Choose a title for the story.

Stage 3

Decide how many characters there are and give them names.

Stage 4

Decide how many scenes it has.

Stage 5

Set this story out as a script in the way that *Survival of the Fittest* shows you.

89

Operation Orpheus 1

The project which is introduced here appears in two other units, Unit 8, Learning from Experience and Unit 9, The World Around You. It will give you the opportunity to explore your ideas in depth, to enjoy drama and to do practical activities. In particular, Operation Orpheus is an opportunity for you to explore what might happen if you had to go underground to survive.

The Threat to the Environment

The threat to the environment is always in the news these days, but what do you really know about it?

One good way of getting ideas moving is to talk together, sharing any idea that comes into your head connected with a topic. Sharing ideas like this is called **brainstorming**. Remember when you brainstorm your ideas, don't worry if they are 'good' or 'bad', just say them.

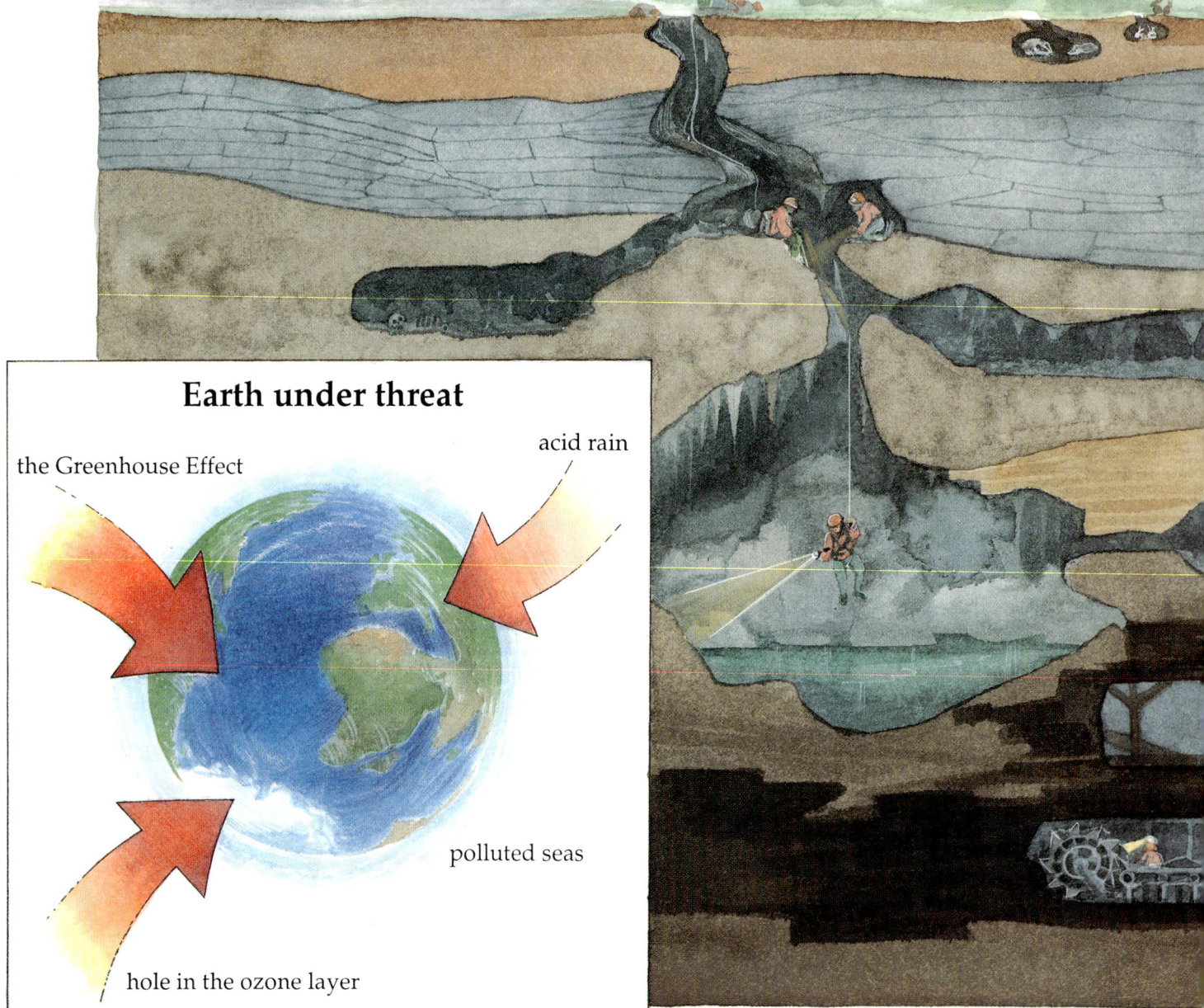

Earth under threat

- the Greenhouse Effect
- acid rain
- polluted seas
- hole in the ozone layer

Operation Orpheus 1

1 In groups, brainstorm together on these things.

◆ the environment
◆ pollution
◆ the ozone layer
◆ the greenhouse effect
◆ acid rain

2 Divide into small groups. Study this diagram which shows some of the things which are damaging the Earth. Decide in your group which of these presents the biggest problem to our survival on Earth. You might need to do some research before you talk about these difficult problems. Make notes so that you can report back to your group.

Operation Orpheus 1

Orpheus

Orpheus was a famous musician. There is a story about him that, when his wife died, he went down into Hell to find her. There he met the king of the Underworld, Pluto. Pluto so liked Orpheus's music that he decided to give Orpheus his wife back. He made Orpheus promise one thing, not to look back until he and his wife returned to the surface of the Earth on pain of death. Unfortunately Orpheus couldn't resist looking back …

1 Imagine that it is a typical day at school until, suddenly, this happens.

Operation Orpheus 1

`10.00`

It is ten o'clock and your class is summoned to the Hall for a very important announcement. When you arrive, there are two official-looking people standing in front of a screen onto which the words **Operation Orpheus** are projected. This is what one of them says.

You might like to get someone in your class, possibly your teacher, to act this out.

Good morning everyone. I have some very important news for you. My name is Professor Friend and this is my colleague Pat Adler.

You may be aware that all has not been going well recently. You may even have read about such things as acid rain or the ozone layer in newspapers or seen programmes about them on the television.

The truth is that we have been treating the Earth so badly that it is about to become impossible to live on its surface any more. You may have noticed that the weather has been very unpredictable recently.

Well, I have to tell you that government scientists have worked out that things have got so bad that we are going to have to go underground in order to survive.

We have been sent to you today because you have to prepare for a sudden evacuation of your school. I am afraid not everyone is going to survive and your class has been chosen to be the first to leave.

In about thirty minutes you will be going down below the surface with us and with your teacher. Parked outside is a vehicle which will take you to the specially prepared lift shaft.

I know this will come as a great shock to you, but I am afraid we have no alternative. In one hour's time, as the sun gains in heat, a series of terrible reactions are going to occur. This will mean that anyone left on Earth will not be able to survive.

Unfortunately it is not possible for you to leave this hall or to contact your friends or family. I am relying on you to be brave and to show calm good sense.

Operation Orpheus 1

10.05

In the next twenty minutes we have to take some very important decisions. Please divide into groups of about six. The first thing you need to decide is what you are going to take with you.

For obvious reasons space is strictly limited. You can only take ten objects per group, plus what ever clothes you are wearing. It will be helpful at this stage if you can choose one of your group to act as spokesperson for the time being.

Please turn out your bags and decide what you think will be most useful to you on your journey.

10.10

Please give these items to your group leader for safekeeping.

In the remaining twenty minutes, please find a quiet space to sit down. I would like each of you to write a brief message to the person or people you are closest to. We can leave these for them so that they, at least, might have the chance to hear from you briefly and know what you are doing.

> Dear Mum and Dad,
> We have been taken from our school by this strange group of scientists. Apparently the world is going to end and we have to

We need to be able to identify each of your groups because you will each be travelling separately. Please decide on a name for your groups, one that will be easy to remember.

Remember, be brave and be cheerful. You are the lucky ones who have the opportunity to create a new world underground.

Operation Orpheus 1

2 This is a role-play exercise.

Only a few minutes ago it was a normal school day. Now you are about to go underground, leaving your family, friends, and everything that is familiar to you. In pairs, decide what you would be feeling now.

Talk about these things.

- what you have been told this morning
- your feelings about the journey
- what you have decided to take with you and why
- anything else that you think might be on your mind at a time like this

The Future Tense

In Unit 3, Making Words Work, there is an introduction to verbs (page 36) and in Unit 5, Imagine What Happened (page 60), the **past** and **present tense** are discussed. The **tense** of the verb tells you **when** something happened. There is a third important tense called the **future**. This is used when writing or talking about things that have yet to happen.

The future tense has a number of forms. The verb often contains the words will or shall. Another common form is the expression 'going to'.

1 This activity is to be done as a role-play.

You are aware that you only have a few more minutes and that there are many unanswered questions. In these last moments you begin to wonder what is going to happen to you and your friends.

In pairs, talk about these points.

- what you think will happen after you have gone underground
- what the main problems will be
- what you will find if you ever return to the surface of the Earth

Reflection

In this Unit you have been practising how to

- listen with concentration
- justify your opinions in a group
- read and perform a play
- set out speech in a play
- use the exclamation mark
- write a simple message

Talk to your friends and your teacher about the things you have been doing in this Unit. Decide how much you have understood and how much progress you have made. Filling in Unit 7 of the Record Sheet on page 126 will also help you think about what you have done in this Unit and the knowledge you are gaining in your English lessons.

Unit 8 Learning From Experience

This Unit gives you the opportunity to

- *talk about characters in a story*
- *play a role*
- *express a point of view*
- *draft your work with less help*
- *use speech in a story*
- *write a short story*
- *keep a diary*

1 In groups, or, if you prefer, on your own, read this short story right through without stopping. If there are things which you do not understand, try and keep going. You can come back later to them.

Becky and the Wheels-and-brake Boys

Even my own cousin Ben was there – riding away, in the ringing of bicycle bells down the road. Every time I came to watch them – see them riding round and round enjoying themselves – they scooted off like crazy on their bikes.

They can't keep doing that. They'll see!

I only want to be with Nat, Aldo, Jimmy and Ben. It's no fair reason they don't want to be with me. Anybody could go off their head for that. Anybody! A girl can not, not, let boys get away with it all the time.

Bother! I have to walk back home, alone. I know total-total that if I had my own bike, the Wheels-and-brake Boys wouldn't treat me like that. I'd just ride away with them, wouldn't I?

Over and over I told my mum I wanted a bike. Over and over she looked at me as if I was crazy. "Becky, d'you think you're a boy? Eh? D'you think you're a boy? In any case, where's the money to come from? Eh?"

Of course I know I'm not a boy. Of course I know I'm not crazy. Of course I know all that's no reason why I can't have a bike. No reason! As soon as I get indoors I'll just have to ask again – ask Mum once more.

96

A Story from Jamaica

At home, indoors, I didn't ask my mum.

It was evening time, but sunshine was still big patches in yards and on housetops. My two younger brothers, Lenny and Vin played marbles in the road. Mum was taking measurements of a boy I knew, for his new trousers and shirt. Mum made clothes for people. Meggie, my sister two years younger than me, was helping Mum on the verandah. Nobody would be pleased with me not helping. I began to help.

Granny-Liz would always stop fanning herself to drink up a glass of iced water. I gave my granny a glass of iced water, there in her rocking-chair. I looked in the kitchen to find shelled coconut pieces to cut into small cubes for the fowls' morning feed. But Granny-Liz had done it. I came and started tidying up bits and pieces of cut-off material around my mum on the floor. My sister got nasty, saying she was already helping Mum. Not a single good thing was happening for me.

With me even being all so thoughtful of Granny's need of a cool drink, she started up some botheration against me.

Listen to Granny-Liz: "Becky, with you moving about me here on the verandah, I hope you don't have any centipedes or scorpions in a jam jar in your pocket."

"No, mam," I said sighing, trying to be calm. "Granny-Liz," I went on, "you forgot. My centipede and scorpion died." All the same, storm broke against me.

"Becky," my mum said. "You know I don't like you wandering off after dinner. Haven't I told you I don't want you keeping company with those awful riding-about bicycle boys? Eh?"

"Yes, mam."

"Those boys are a menace. Riding bicycles on sidewalks and narrow paths together, ringing bicycle bells and braking at people's feet like wild bulls charging anybody, they're heading for trouble."

"They're the Wheels-and-brake Boys, mam."

"The what?"

"The Wheels-and-brake Boys."

"Oh! Given themselves a name as well, have they? Well, Becky, answer this. How d'you always manage to look like you've just escaped from a hair-pulling battle? Eh? And don't I tell you not to break the back down and wear your canvas shoes like slippers? Don't you ever hear what I say?"

"Yes, mam."

"D'you want to end up a field labourer? Like where your father used to be overseer?"

"No, mam."

"Well, Becky, will you please go off and do your homework?"

Everybody did everything to stop me. I was allowed no chance whatsoever. No chance to talk to Mum about the bike I dream of day and night! And I knew exactly the bike I wanted. I wanted a bike like Ben's bike. Oh, I wished I still had even my scorpion on a string to run up and down somebody's back!

I answered my mum. "Yes, mam." I went off into Meg's and my bedroom.

I sat down at the little table, as well I might. Could homework stay in anybody's head in broad daylight outside? No. Could I keep a bike like Ben's out of my head? Not one bit. That bike took me all over the place. My beautiful bike jumped every log, every rock, every fence. My beautiful bike did everything cleverer than a clever

97

A Story from Jamaica

cowboy's horse, with me in the saddle. And the bell, the bell was such a glorious gong of a ring!

If Dad was alive I could talk to him. If Dad was alive he'd give me money for the bike like a shot.

I sighed. It was amazing what a sigh could do. I sighed and tumbled on a great idea. Tomorrow evening I'd get Shirnette to come with me. Both of us together would be sure to get the boys interested to teach us to ride. Wow! With Shirnette they can't just ride away!

Next day at school everything went sour. For the first time, Shirnette and me had a real fight, because of what I hated most.

Shirnette brought a cockroach to school in a shoe-polish tin. At playtime she opened the tin and let the cockroach fly into my blouse. Pure panic and disgust nearly killed me. I crushed up the cockroach in my clothes and practically ripped my blouse off, there in open sunlight. Oh the smell of a cockroach is the nastiest ever to block your nose! I started running with my blouse to go and wash it. Twice I had to stop and be sick.

I washed away the crushed cockroach stain from my blouse. Then the stupid Shirnette had to come into the toilet, falling about laughing. All right, I knew the cockroach treatment was for the time when I made my centipede on a string crawl up Shirnette's back. But you put fair-is-fair aside. I just barged into Shirnette.

When it was all over I had on a wet blouse, but Shirnette had one on too.

Then going home with the noisy flock of children from school I had ever such a new, new idea. If Mum thought I was scruffy, Nat, Aldo, Jimmy and Ben might think so too. I didn't like that.

A Story from Jamaica

After dinner, I combed my hair in the bedroom. Mum did her machining on the verandah. Meggie helped Mum. Granny sat there, wishing she could take on any job, as usual.

I told Mum I was going to make up a quarrel with Shirnette. I went, but my friend wouldn't speak to me, let alone come out to keep me company. I stood alone and watched the Wheels-and-brake Boys again.

This time the boys didn't race away past me. I stood leaning against the tall coconut palm tree. People passed up and down. The nearby main road was busy with traffic. But I didn't mind. I watched the boys. Riding round and round the big Flame-tree, Nat, Aldo, Jimmy and Ben looked marvellous.

At first each boy rode round the tree alone. Then each boy raced each other round the tree, going round three times. As he won, the winner rang his bell on and on, till he stopped panting and could laugh and talk properly. Next, most reckless and fierce, all the boys raced against each other. And, leaning against their bicycles, talking and joking, the boys popped soft drinks open, drank and ate chipped bananas.

I walked up to Nat, Aldo, Jimmy and Ben and said, "Can somebody teach me to ride?"

"Why don't you stay indoors and learn to cook and sew and wash clothes?" Jimmy said.

I grinned. "I know all that already," I said. "And one day perhaps I'll even be mum to a boy child, like all of you. Can you cook and sew and wash clothes, Jimmy? All I want is to learn to ride. I want you to teach me."

I didn't know why I said what I said. But everybody went silent and serious.

One after the other, Nat, Aldo, Jimmy and Ben got on to their bikes and rode off. I wasn't at

99

A Story from Jamaica

all cross with them. I only wanted to be riding out of the playground with them. I knew they'd be heading into the town to have ice-cream and things and talk and laugh.

Mum was sitting alone on the verandah. She sewed buttons on to a white shirt she'd made. I sat down next to Mum. Straightaway, "Mum," I said, "I still want to have a bike badly."

"Oh, Becky, you still have that foolishness in your head? What am I going to do?"

Mum talked with some sympathy. Mum knew I was honest. "I can't get rid of it, mam," I said.

Mum stopped sewing. "Becky," she said, staring in my face, "how many girls around here do you see with bicycles?"

"Janice Gordon has a bike," I reminded her.

"Janice Gordon's dad has acres and acres of coconuts and bananas, with a business in the town as well."

I knew Mum was just about to give in. Then my granny had to come out on to the verandah and interfere. Listen to that Granny-Liz. "Becky, I heard your mother tell you over and over she can't afford to buy you a bike. Yet you keep on and on. Child, you're a girl."

"But I don't want a bike because I'm a girl."

"D'you want it because you feel like a boy?" Granny said.

"No. I only want a bike because I want it and want it and want it."

Granny just carried on. "A tomboy's like a whistling woman and a crowing hen, who can only come to a bad end. D'you understand?"

I didn't want to understand. I knew Granny's speech was an awful speech. I went and sat down with Lenny and Vin, who were making a kite.

By Saturday morning I felt real sorry for Mum. I could see Mum really had it hard for money. I had to try and help. I knew anything of Dad's – anything – would be worth a great mighty hundred dollars.

I found myself in the centre of town, going through the busy Saturday crowd. I hoped Mum wouldn't be too cross. I went into the fire station. With lots of luck I came face to face with a round

A Story from Jamaica

face man in uniform. He talked to me. "Little miss, can I help you?"

I told him I'd like to talk to the head man.

He took me into the office and gave me a chair. I sat down. I opened out my brown paper parcel. I showed him my dad's sun helmet. I told him I thought it would make a good fireman's hat. I wanted to sell the helmet for some money towards a bike, I told him.

The fireman laughed a lot. I began to laugh too. The fireman put me in a car and drove me back home.

Mum's eyes popped to see me bringing home the fireman. The round face fireman laughed at my adventure. Mum laughed too, which was really good. The fireman gave Mum my dad's hat back. Then, mystery, mystery, Mum sent me outside while they talked.

My mum was only a little cross with me. Then – mystery and more mystery – my mum took me with the fireman in his car to his house.

The fireman brought out what? A bicycle! A beautiful, shining bicycle! His nephew's bike. His nephew had been taken away, all the way to America. The bike had been left with the fireman-uncle for him to sell it. And the good kind fireman-uncle decided we could have the bike – on small payments. My mum looked uncertain. But, in a big, big way the fireman knew it was all right. And Mum smiled a little. My mum had good sense to know it was all right. My mum took the bike from the fireman Mister Dean.

And guess what? Seeing my bike much, much newer than his, my cousin Ben's eyes popped with envy. But – he took on the big job. He taught me to ride. Then he taught Shirnette.

I ride into town with the Wheels-and-brake Boys now. When she can borrow a bike, Shirnette comes too. We all sit together. We have patties and ice-cream and drink drinks together. We talk and joke. We ride about, all over the place.

And, again, guess what? Fireman Mister Dean became our best friend, and Mum's especially. He started coming round almost every day.

James Berry

Who's Who in the Story?

1. There are three generations of characters in this story. Which characters are in Becky's family? Which are in the gang? What other characters are there? What do you find out about each one?

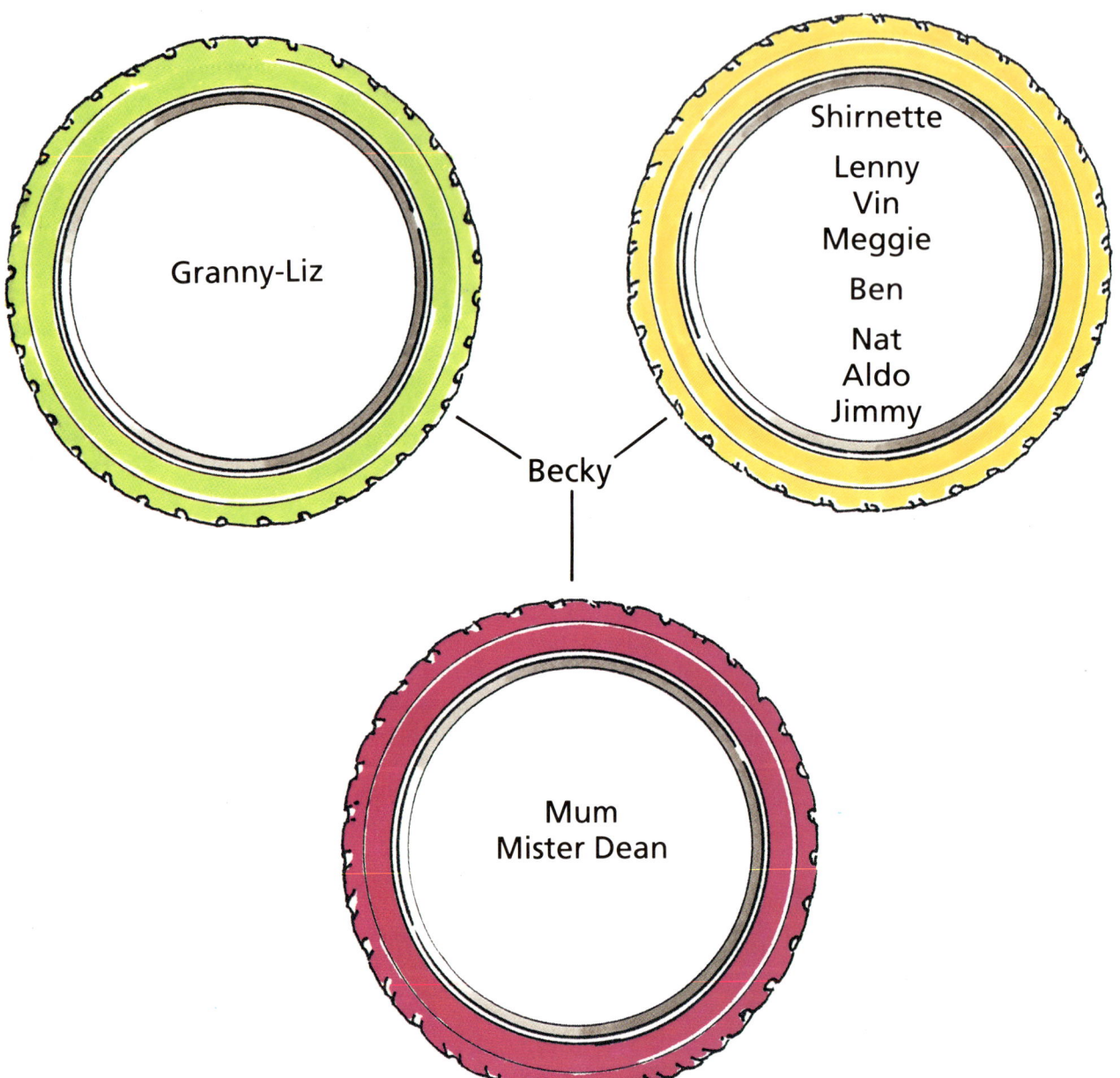

2. In pairs, choose four characters from the story. Decide about these points.
   - how old you think they are
   - what you learn about them from what they say
   - what you learn about them from what they do
   - what you most remember about them

3. Apart from Becky, which character do you feel you know best by the end of the story?

When you write a story you have to take a number of decisions. One of these is who your characters will be. Your characters will not all be equally important. Normally you will have to decide who is your main character. For example, in this story James

Who's Who in the Story?

Berry has chosen to make the main character a girl called Becky. All the other characters are seen through her eyes and they help you to understand something about Becky.

Granny-Liz

1 Look at these statements that Granny-Liz makes. Do you think Becky agrees with them? What do you think Becky's views are?

Becky, I heard your mother tell you over and over she can't afford to buy you a bike. Yet you keep on and on. Child, you're a girl.

A tomboy's like a whistling woman and a crowing hen, who can only come to a bad end.

2 This is an opportunity to role play. In pairs, imagine one of you is Granny-Liz and the other is Mum. Becky has been pestering both of you all day to try and persuade you to buy her a bike. You each have different reasons for not letting her have one. Have a conversation about this problem.

Shirnette

1 Look again at the paragraphs in the story dealing with the quarrel between Shirnette and Becky.

2 In pairs, discuss why Becky and Shirnette fall out with each other.

Do you ever quarrel or fight with your friends? If so, what kinds of things do you argue about?

3 Imagine you are Becky. Write a poem about your quarrel with Shirnette. Or you could write more generally about friendship and quarrels.

Who's Who in the Story?

The Wheels-and-brake Boys

'They're the Wheels-and-brake Boys.'
'Oh! Given themselves a name as well, have they?'

1 In pairs, discuss the importance of the gang, the Wheels-and-brake Boys, in the story. You might like to talk through these ideas.

- Why does Becky want to belong to the gang?
- Do they want her to join?
- What are your own experiences of gangs?
- What other good names for gangs have you heard of?
- What other stories do you know in which there is a gang?
- Why do you think young people like to belong to a gang?
- Do you think gangs are important to older people? Can you think of any examples?

Mister Dean

1 This is a role-play. In the story Becky goes to try and sell Mister Dean her dad's sun helmet to raise money.

What do you think he thinks when she arrives at the fire station?

Why do you think he decides to help her?

2 **Then, mystery, mystery, Mum sent me outside while they talked.**

What do you think Mum and Mister Dean said? In pairs, make up their conversation.

Copy your role-play out as a script, to be acted out by someone else in your class.

3 Imagine you are Becky. Write a letter to Mister Dean, thanking him for the bicycle. You could tell him what you plan to do now you have a bike and how much it means to you.

Who's Who in the Story?

What's Behind the Story?

1 In groups, decide who makes each of these statements. What does each statement tell you about the person who makes it?

A girl can not, not, let boys get away with it all the time.

Becky, d'you think you're a boy? Eh?

Why don't you stay indoors and learn to cook and sew and wash clothes?

And one day perhaps I'll even be mum to a boy child, like all of you.

How many girls around here do you see with bicycles?

But I don't want a bike because I'm a girl.

One of the things Becky and the Wheels-and-brake-Boys **is about, is different views of girls and boys and what each should or should not do.**

2 In the past girls and boys could only take part in certain activities. For example, it used to be uncommon for boys to cook and girls to play football. In a small group, discuss which, if any, of the activities below are more popular with either girls or boys.

football

making model aeroplanes

flying kites

buying clothes

climbing trees

listening to pop music

hockey

swimming

keeping insects

cooking

embroidery

shopping for food

computer games

riding bicycles

watching television

Why do you think that some of these are popular with boys or girls?

3 Whether you are a girl or a boy says what **gender** you are. Using an activity from the list or one that you have thought of yourself, design a poster to encourage the other gender to take part in it. Include a slogan or sentence to go with it which you think people will remember.

Painting Pictures with Words

James Berry does not just write short stories. If you look back to Unit 3, Making Words Work, on page 34, you will see that he is the author of the poem *Mum Dad and Me*. Like most writers he chooses his words carefully. He likes to get the most out of each word.

Granny-Liz would always stop fanning herself to drink a glass of water.

I hope you haven't got any centipedes or scorpions in a jam jar in your pocket.

Painting Pictures with Words

1 In pairs, study the first five paragraphs of the story again.

2 Look at the very first sentence again, in particular. When you read the first seven words, why did you think James Berry started off with the word **Even**? Where did you think there was? Does this way of starting make you think that you are in the middle of something? Did it make you want to read on?

3 Had you heard the expression **in the ringing of bicycle bells** before? James Berry probably made it up, or if it was something that he had heard people saying, chose to include it here. What do you think it means? How would you have put this?

4 Look at paragraph five. James Berry has deliberately used language which comes from things people say when talking to each other casually. Which words in it have you not read before? What do you think they mean?

5 Look at the length of his sentences. How many words are there in each? Look at the length of his paragraphs. What do you notice? Do you find this an interesting way to write? Does it change the way you read the story? Does it make it dull or more exciting? How?

There is no one set way to write a story. You have to develop your own style and the style you use for one story may be different from the one you use for another. As well as using a variety of words often used in speech, James Berry also writes in a more formal way when he chooses to.

> Then going home with the noisy flock of children from school I had ever such a new, new idea.

107

Painting Pictures with Words

1 In pairs, look at page 97. Granny-Liz is described in ways like those you have met in Unit 5, Imagine What Happened (see page 54). You also find out something about Becky's situation.

2 In small groups, go through the story carefully.

Choose two sections of about five or ten lines each that you like or that you think you have things to say about. Try and choose two different sections. For example you might select one piece with someone speaking and another that is a description. You might like to include the ending as one of your pieces.

Present your two extracts to another group in your class, explaining clearly why you have chosen them.

Writing Your Own Short Story

1 Write a short story about a group of characters. Your story should focus on one of these characters in particular. It should also, like the one you have just read, make your readers think! (For example, in *Becky and the Wheels-and-Brake Boys*, readers are encouraged to think about how girls should behave and whether they should ride bicycles.)

You are already familiar with the essential features of drafting. On the pages which follow you will be learning about this technique in more detail. There is no one set way of drafting a story: each writer is different. The important thing is to ask yourself a series of questions as you write and to be prepared to make changes to your work.

Painting Pictures with Words

Starting Writing

Question 1: Why are you writing and who are you writing for?

It is important to be honest about this. For example, in this case you have been told that you should write a certain type of story. In your English lessons, you will sometimes have a completely free choice, and sometimes you will be given some direction from your teacher or from materials you are using.

Here you need to decide who you are writing for. It could be for a class anthology, for yourself, for your teacher, for a friend or for anyone you choose.

Question 2: What are you going to write about?

Sometimes the type of story you choose will help you here. For example, if you choose to write a horror story or a story about yourself (as in Unit 1, Starting Out, on page 9) or a story about animals, then you will be thinking about this when you decide what happens.

Here you need to decide what the point of your story is going to be. Is it going to be about growing up, about some kind of lucky escape, about an issue? Many writers find this one of the most difficult stages. It is tempting to say

'I just don't know what to write ... I'm stuck.'

Many people find it helpful to jot down on a planning page any ideas they have so far. In Unit 1, Starting Out, page 9 and Unit 4 page 48, there are two examples of plans that you might like to use. Try and work out at least how it will start, some of the important events in it and, possibly, how it will end. Often a partner or teacher can help at this point.

Another way is to talk through your story with a partner and share ideas by brainstorming. Remember brainstorming means sharing ideas on the topic quickly, as they come to you, without worrying about whether they are good or bad.

Question 3: Where are you going to set it?

The story you have just read was set in Jamaica, because this is the area the writer knew best. He had in his head memories, sounds, pictures and words from this island. Often you will find it easier to picture a setting that you know well, even if you are going to make up your characters. Sometimes, though, you will want to make this up as well.

Here you need to decide whether to write about a place you know or to make up the setting. If you decide to make it up, start to jot down ideas at this stage. Sometimes it is helpful to draw a map or a room plan.

Question 4: Who are you going to include?

You have just read a story with eleven characters in it, although you only get to know three or four well.

For this story you have been asked to write mainly about one character in particular. Will it be a boy or a girl? Interestingly, James Berry chose to write about a member of the opposite gender, a girl of about your own age.

Here you need to decide how many characters to include. Select names for them and begin to jot down ideas about them. Sometimes it is helpful to write out a family tree.

Painting Pictures with Words

Composing

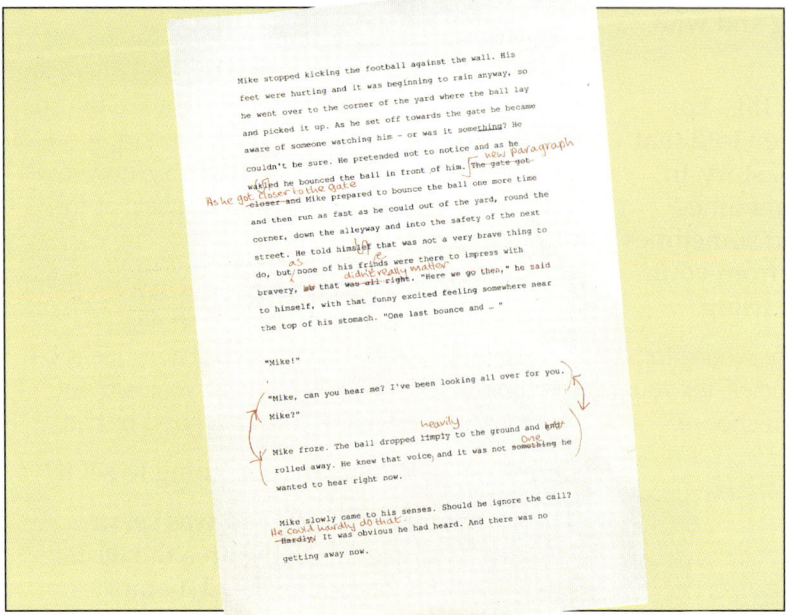

Question 5: What style are you going to use?

From the decisions you have already made, the answer to this question should already be becoming clearer.

How much speech will you include? Do you know how to set it out in a story? (In case you need reminding, there is some advice at the end of the description of this stage and more in *Taking Shape*, the second book in the **Opportunities** series.)

Whose eyes will you see the story through? For example, in the story you have been reading, James Berry sees it through Becky's, but you might want to tell it from your own point of view as the writer.

How will you start? By this stage in your development as a writer you will have moved on from the Once upon a time approach! Even so, many young writers find starting to write a draft very hard.

You could try beginning in the middle of things, as in *Becky and the Wheels-and-brake Boys*, where it seems as if the problem about Becky's bicycle has been going on for some time. Alternatively you could start with someone talking, in the middle of a conversation perhaps, or calling something out.

Here you will need to decide answers to all these questions. You will also have to decide on the length of your sentences.

At this stage the important thing is to start writing your first draft and not to worry about how it looks or whether you have got all the answers.

If you can use a wordprocessor for this stage it will be very helpful, but it is not essential.

Revising

Question 6: Who can help me improve my writing?

As soon as you have started writing, there are many people who can help you.

Someone else in your class
This is often the best way of getting instant advice.

Your teacher
S/he can ask you more questions to help you and point you to an area which you might be able to improve on.

Your family
Sometimes you may not want to show another member of your family what you are writing, but on many occasions you may be grateful for the help.

You need to decide what to change and what to keep as you draft, and possibly write out your draft again.

Painting Pictures with Words

Proof-reading

Question 7: Is it set out properly?

At this stage it becomes more important to improve your presentation.

Use a dictionary to check on spellings.

Use a thesaurus to give you ideas for new words.

Check that all of your sentences make complete sense, begin with a capital letter and end with a full stop or other punctuation mark. You may like to look back to Unit 2, Picking Up Clues (see page 22) and Unit 6, Getting to Grips with Language (see pages 66 and 67) to help you.

How to set out speech in a story

There are three things to remember.

Anything a person says in a story should be put in speech marks. For example,

> 'I can't get rid of it, mam,' I said.

Every time a new person speaks, you start a new line.

Before the second speech mark, you must have one of the following punctuation marks

> full stop (.')
>
> comma (,')
>
> exclamation mark (!')
>
> question mark (?')

You will find that single (') speech marks are normally used in books, but double (") speech marks are just as correct, too, and double speech marks are the speech marks taught to you when you are learning about the different marks of punctuation.

Make sure that your sentences are organised into paragraphs and that these are properly set out.

Make sure that you know which tense you are using and why. Look back at Unit 5, Imagine What Happened (see page 60) and Unit 7, Thinking About the Future (see page 95), if you are unsure about this.

For all of these activities you may need help to begin with.

Publishing

Question 8: When is it finished?

This depends on the answer to Question 1 on page 109. If you are writing your story to include it in a class magazine, your editor may want it typed or written on a wordprocessor. If you are planning to display it, a handwritten copy might look more individual.

Perhaps you want to illustrate it?

Before you begin your final copy make sure you are presenting your work in the most suitable form.

Read each others' stories. How do these stories differ from other stories you have written?

Operation Orpheus 2

This is the second part of the project which starts in Unit 7, Thinking About the Future (see page 92). It was left at the point where you and your class were about to be taken underground on a journey of survival.

The Journey Down

Day 1 A.M.

Return to the groups you were in for the first part of Operation Orpheus. You have a number of decisions to take about your progress so far. You are now 80 metres underground at the base of a lift shaft. Beside you is a pile of equipment which has been specially prepared for life underground.

Each group has just been given this sheet of advice to help you choose what equipment you will take on your journey. Remember that you are already carrying a number of personal items and that it will not be necessary for every member of the group to have the same equipment.

Each member of the group should select the six items from the picture opposite that you think would be most useful at this stage. There will be opportunities later on to collect extra items of equipment.

Each individual should present their selection to the group, who must all agree the final selection. If you can't agree, your group leader should have the final say.

OPERATION ORPHEUS

Advice Sheet 1

1 All personal items should be neatly packed in your rucksack.

2 Individual articles can be waterproofed by being packed into plastic sheets or plastic screw-topped containers.

3 Each individual should carry some high energy foods.

4 Each group must have at least two thermos flasks.

5 Each group must have a first-aid kit.

6 Each group must have a whistle.

7 Each group must have a length of climbing rope and a number of harnesses.

8 Each individual must have a head torch and a sleeping bag.

Operation Orpheus 2

Operation Orpheus 2

Underground Worlds

You might not have been underground before, but many other people have. Here are some photographs showing the conditions that people have found hundreds of metres below the surface of the Earth.

Day 1 P.M.

You have been travelling through caves similar to the ones in the photographs. You are now 200 metres underground and close to Base Camp. It has been a long day.

You have stopped to decide whether to go on for another two hours or to sleep where you are. Professor Friend has just stood up and begun to speak to you.

Well done everybody. I'm very impressed by the way you've all pulled together today. I know it's been very strange and for some of you rather frightening and I'm sorry that I had to force some of you on. I hope you see that I had your best interests at heart.

Operation Orpheus 2

I know you are now very tired. Tomorrow we will be arriving at Base Camp. Before you go to sleep tonight I would very much like you to record exactly what your group has done today. I think you'll understand that without light it's very easy to lose track of time. For this reason it's essential that you all keep a diary.

I suggest you begin by talking through in your group what you did when you left school, the journey down in the lift, and the last part of the day in the caves.

Operation Orpheus 2

Starting to Live Underground

Professor Friend continues with what she has to say to you.

When you have got the day clear in your heads, either make a group record or write your own diary entry about it, as a record for us to keep track of events and time.

I noticed that one of you chose to bring a book called Z for Zachariah *with you. You might find it helpful to look at the beginning of it and see how a diary can be kept. Like you, the girl in the book was trying to survive a disaster.*

Working as a team

Day 2 P.M.

You have now reached Base Camp. Pat Adler, Professor Friend's colleague, has called you all together for a meeting and now begins to speak.

Welcome to Base Camp. As you can see, a great deal of preparation has already gone into this operation. However it is now that the hard work really begins. So far you have relied on us. From now on we will be relying more and more on you. Down here we are all equals. Each of us has things to offer. The important thing is to pull together as a team.

Z for Zachariah

May 20th

I am afraid.

Someone is coming.

That is, I think someone is coming, though I am not sure, and I pray that I am wrong. I went into the church and prayed all this morning. I sprinkled water in front of the altar, and put some flowers on it, violets and dogwood.

But there is smoke. For three days there has been smoke, not like the time before. That time, last year, it rose in a great cloud a long way away, and stayed in the sky for two weeks. A forest fire in the dead woods, and then it rained and the smoke stopped. But this time it is a thin column, like a pole, not very high.

And the column has come three times, each time in the late afternoon. At night I cannot see it, and in the morning, it is gone. But each afternoon it comes again, and it is nearer. At first it was behind Claypole Ridge, and I could see only the top of it, the smallest smudge. I thought it was a cloud, except that it was too grey, the wrong colour, and then I thought: there are no clouds anywhere else. I got the binoculars and saw that it was narrow and straight; it was smoke from a small fire. When we used to go in the truck, Claypole Ridge was fifteen miles, though it looks closer, and the smoke was coming from behind that.

Beyond Claypole Ridge there is Ogdentown, about ten miles further. But there is no one left alive in Ogdentown.

I know, because after the war ended, and all the telephones went dead, my father, my brother Joseph and Cousin David went in the truck to find out what was happening, and the first place they went was Ogdentown. They went early in the morning; Joseph and David were really excited, but Father looked serious.

When they came back it was dark. Mother had been worrying – they took so long – so we were glad to see the truck lights finally coming over Burden Hill, six miles away. They looked like beacons. They were the only lights anywhere, except in the house – no other cars had come down all day. We knew it was the truck because one of the lights, the left one, always blinked when it went over a bump. It came up to the house and they got out; the boys weren't excited any more. They looked scared, and my father looked sick. Maybe he was beginning to be sick, but mainly I think he was distressed.

My mother looked up at him as he climbed down. "What did you find?"

He said, "Bodies. Just dead bodies. They're all dead."

"All?"

We went inside the house where the lamps were lit, the two boys following, not saying anything. My father sat down. "Terrible," he said, and again, "terrible, terrible. We drove around, looking. We blew the horn. Then we went to the church and rang the bell. You can hear it five miles away. We waited for two hours, but nobody came. I went into a couple of houses – the Johnsons', the Peters' – they were all in there, all dead. There were dead birds all over the streets."

My brother Joseph began to cry. He was fourteen. I think I had not heard him cry for six years.

May 21st

It is coming closer. Today it was almost on top of the ridge, though not quite, because when I looked with the

We did not have a lot of time when we selected your class and we have had to rely on what your teachers told us. Everyone knows that this is only part of it. We'd like to hear your story.

What we want you to produce is a Group Profile. To do this you are going to need to be as honest as you can about your individual strengths and weaknesses, what you like and what you dislike and what you have to offer our enterprise. Remember, this is not just an individual effort. We want you to work together as a team. What you have to say about your group has to be agreed by everybody in it.

You now have half an hour to fill in the individual parts of your Group Profile and for the group to agree each person's details.

OPERATION ORPHEUS

Name

Skills/Talents
(e.g. First Aid Badge, Duke of Edinburgh Award, etc.)

Experience
(e.g. caving, climbing, residential holidays etc.)

Hobbies/Interests

Strengths

Weaknesses

Likes

Dislikes

Special Notes

binoculars I could not see the flame, but still only the smoke – rising very fast, not far above the fire. I know where it is: at the crossroads. Just on the other side of the ridge, the east–west highway, the Dean Town Road, crosses our road. It is Route number nine, a State highway, bigger than our road, which is County road 793. He has stopped there and is deciding whether to follow number nine or come over the ridge. I say *he* because that is what I think of, though it could be *they* or even *she*. But I think it is he. If he decides to follow the highway he will go away, and everything will be all right again. Why would he come back? But if he comes to the top of the ridge, he is sure to come down here, because he will see the green leaves. On the other side of the ridge, even on the other side of Burden Hill, there are no leaves; everything is dead.

There are some things I need to explain. One is why I am afraid. Another is why I am writing in this composition book, which I got from Klein's store a mile up the road.

I took the book and a supply of ballpoint pens back in February. By then the last radio station, a very faint one that I could hear only at night, had stopped broadcasting. It had been dead for about three or four months. I say *about*, and that is one reason I got the book: because I discovered I was forgetting when things happened, and sometimes even *whether* things happened or not. Another reason I got it is that I thought writing in it might be like having someone to talk to, and if I read it back later it would be like someone talking to me. But the truth is I haven't written in it much after all, because there isn't much to write about.

from *Z for Zachariah*, Robert C. O'Brien

The leader should then tell the whole party what his or her group has to contribute, but s/he should try to avoid simply going through each person, individually.

Reflection

In this Unit you have been practising how to

- talk about characters in a story
- put across information and ideas effectively
- express a point of view about a story
- understand how a writer's choice of words affects the reader
- re-draft writing in the light of discussion
- set out speech in a story
- plan and write a complete short story
- keep a diary
- take decisions in a group

Talk to your friends and your teacher about the things you have been doing in this Unit. Decide how much you have understood and how much progress you have made. Filling in Unit 8 of the Record Sheet on page 126 will also help you think about what you have done in this Unit and the knowledge you are gaining in your English lessons.

Unit 9 The World Around You

This Unit gives you the opportunity to
- *read in order to find out more information*
- *design a pamphlet*
- *answer questions*
- *play a role*
- *talk about your experiences*
- *solve problems in a group*
- *develop a storyline*

1 Study this information about the environment.

2 What kind of organisation do you think produced this? What is your evidence?

Use your school library to look up anything that you do not understand or wish to find out more about.

How many of these ideas are familiar to you? Look back to the brainstorming exercise in Unit 7, Thinking About the Future, on page 90.

Which of the following statements are true and which are false?

Nothing is changing in the world about us

Cutting down trees in the Amazon is bad for the atmosphere

Sea-levels are falling all round the world

Sea-levels are rising all round the world

Using refrigerators keeps the world's atmosphere cooler

There will be no changes to the Earth's weather for the next 200 years

If we don't make some changes soon, famines and droughts will increase

3 Make up some true/false statements of your own for other members of your group to decide on. The aim of this is to help them take in some of the main points of this complex information.

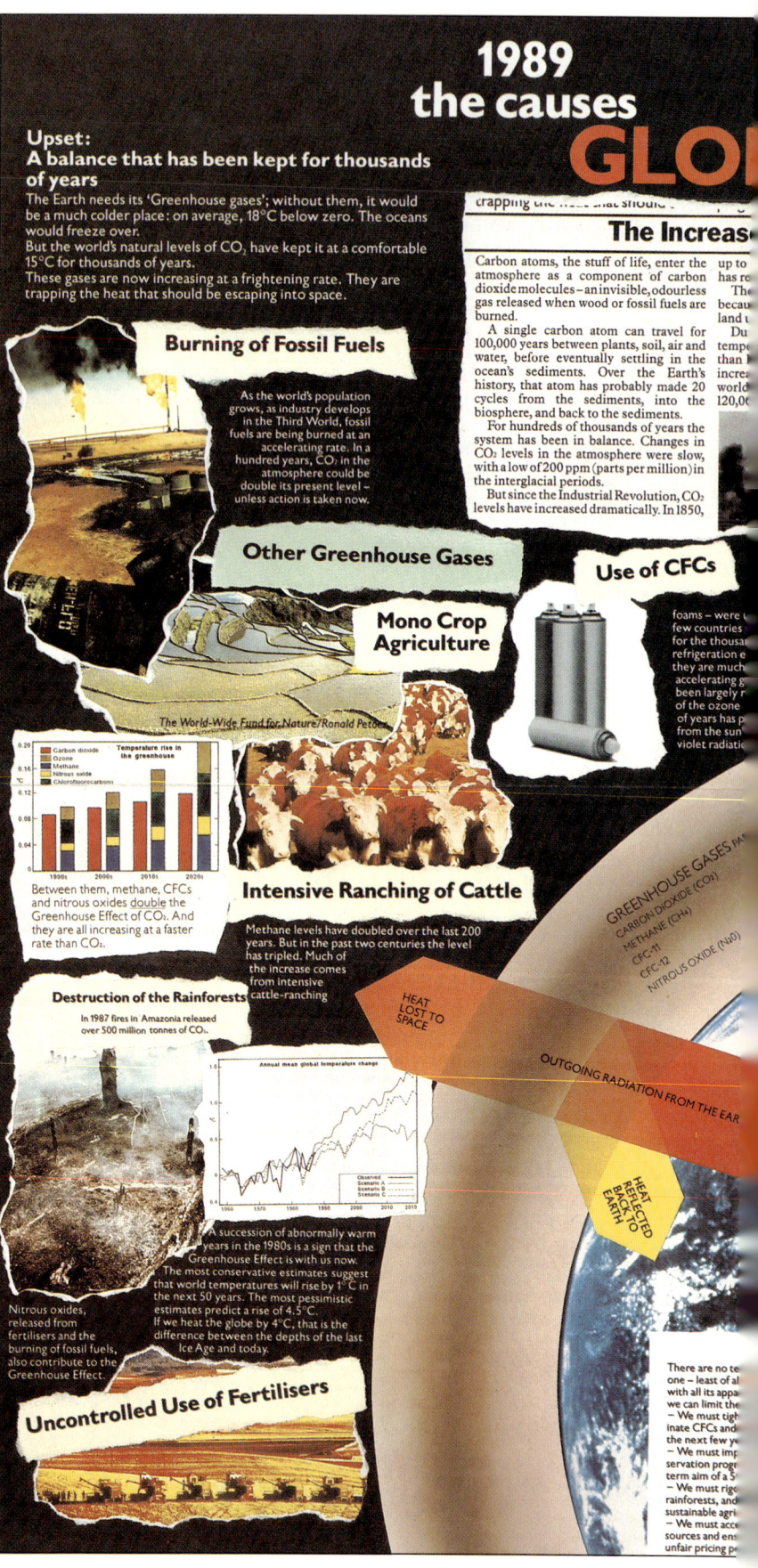

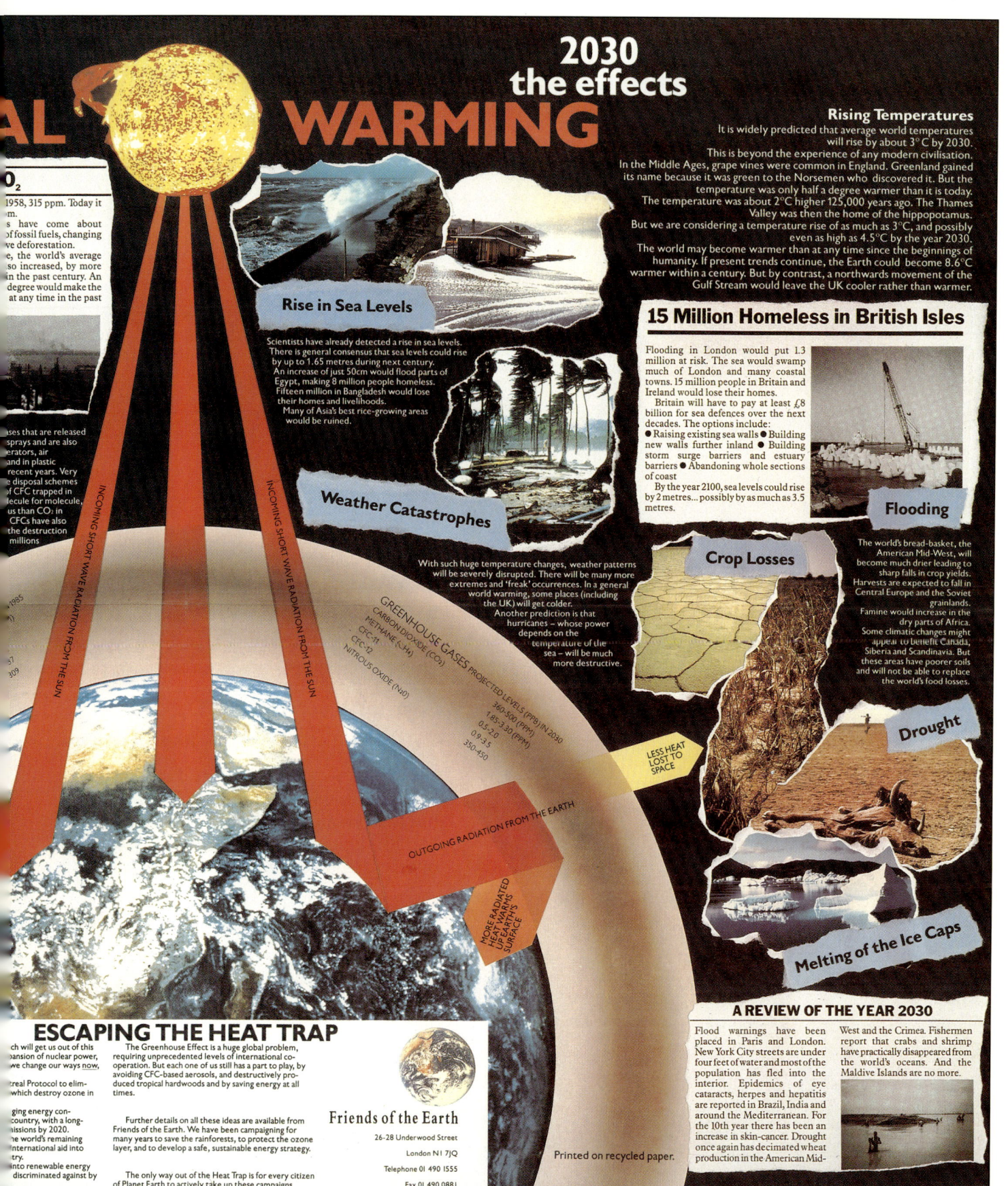

Pressure for Change

1 Study this poem carefully.

Poisoned Talk

Who killed cock robin?
I, said the worm,
I did him great harm.
He died on the branch of a withered tree
From the acid soil that poisoned me.

Who killed the heron?
I, mouthed the fish,
With my tainted flesh
I killed tern, duck and drake,
All the birds of the lake.

Who killed the lake?
I, boasted Industry,
I poisoned with mercury
Fish, plant and weed
To pamper men's greed.

Who killed the flowers?
I, moaned the wind,
I prowl unconfined,
Blowing acid rain
Over field, flood and fen.

Who killed the forest?
I ensured that it died,
Said sulphur dioxide,
And all life within it,
From earth worm to linnet.

Raymond Wilson

This poem is called a **parody.** A parody is an imitation or copy of another piece of writing, but it is not an exact copy. It is usually done to make a point, sometimes a funny one or, as in this case, a very serious one.

Pressure for Change

In fact the poem you have just read is a parody of this well-known nursery rhyme.

Who Killed Cock Robin?

Who killed Cock Robin?
I, said the sparrow,
With my bow and arrow,
I killed Cock Robin.

Who saw him die?
I, said the fly,
With my little eye,
I saw him die.

Who caught his blood?
I, said the fish,
With my little dish,
I caught his blood.

Who will make his shroud?
I, said the beetle,
With my thread and needle,
I'll make his shroud.

Who'll dig his grave?
I, said the owl,
With my pick and shovel,
I'll dig his grave.

Traditional

2 What is the message of the first poem?

What do you think the nursery rhyme is about? In both there are difficult words which you may need to look up.

What areas do Raymond Wilson and Friends Of The Earth agree on?

Both are trying to make a point about the environment. Which method do you prefer? Explain your reasons.

3 Choose a subject that concerns you. It may be to do with the environment or it may be to do with some other issue you feel strongly about.

Stage 1
Do some research on your chosen topic.

Stage 2
Either design a pamphlet with information presented as it is on pages 118 and 119 or write a poem to make your point. You might like to try writing your own parody. You could use *Who Killed Cock Robin?* or a nursery rhyme, song or poem of your choice.

Operation Orpheus 3

This is the third part of the project which started in Unit 7, Thinking About the Future, on page 92, and continued in Unit 8, Learning from Experience, on page 112.

Day 15 A.M.

You have now been living underground for two weeks. At first it was very difficult becoming used to having no natural light. It was also hard to adapt to a diet of dried food and sterilised water. For some people it is all beginning to be too much.

You have just had another boring breakfast. You are about to have your morning meeting to decide each group's tasks for the day. This is what the Professor says.

Good morning everybody. I hope you all slept rather better than I did! I was very pleased to be able to speak to one of your groups last night. In fact the ideas we discussed were spinning around in my head for much of the night.

It may surprise you to know that I share many of your fears. I am missing my home, my family and above all my comfortable bed! However, as a scientist I can reassure you that what we are trying to do is not impossible. Back in 1969 a famous caver called Milutin Veljkovic spent a whole year underground in a cave in Yugoslavia. It can be done. But it is difficult and we are human.

Today I suggest we do no work, but instead try to enjoy ourselves a little and to cheer ourselves up.

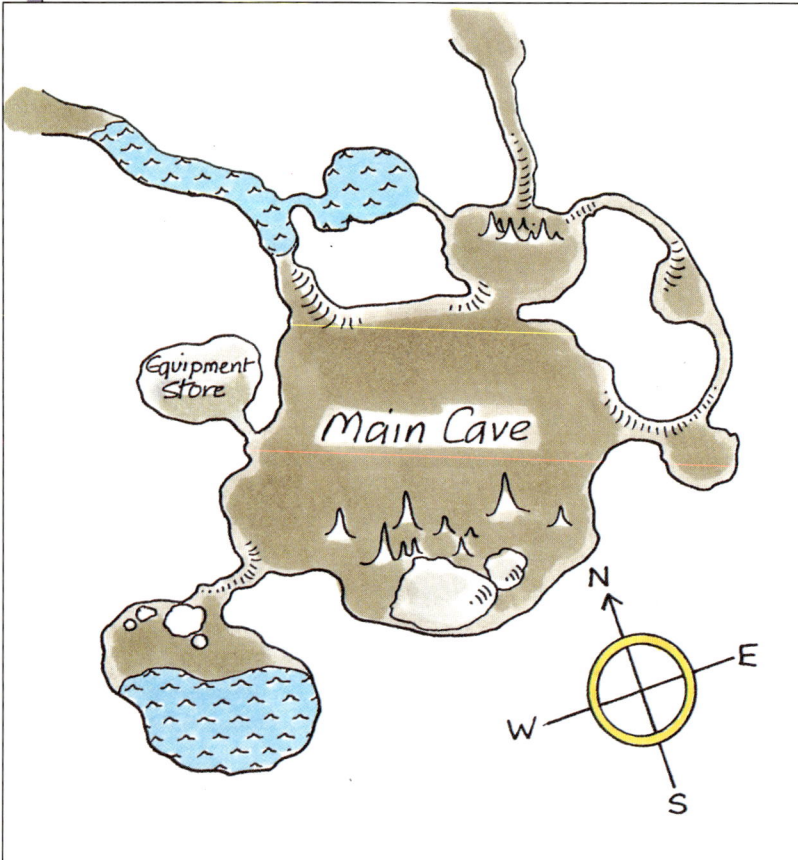

1 When the Professor has finished speaking split into small groups to do this role-play exercise. Make up a scene in which you act out how you think you would be feeling at this stage. Talk about these things.

- what has happened in the last two weeks (look back at Operation Orpheus 1 (page 92) and 2 (page 112))
- what you are missing
- what you think about the way things are being organised
- what your chances of survival are
- whether you should stay with the main group or go off on your own
- whether you trust the Professor

Day 15 P.M.

You have now seen all the plays and it has been a pleasant change. In the afternoon you have been given some free time and your group decides to explore the area around Base Camp. Each group has been issued with a very basic map.

2 Make a copy of the map and mark on it the main landmarks of your new life underground. Include these things.

sleeping quarters
eating area
cooking area
rubbish dump

What other necessary information must you include?

Your group decides to explore the area around Base Camp in order to make a more detailed map of it. So that you can cover more ground, you decide to split into two smaller groups. Each group will then make one map of what they discover.

However, while exploring, one of your group has an accident.

3 Decide who is injured. Decide what has happened to her or him. Decide how s/he is hurt.

What are you going to do? There are three of you, one of whom is now looking very poorly. You were warned by the Professor about the importance of safety underground. She gave you an Advice Sheet with this information on it.

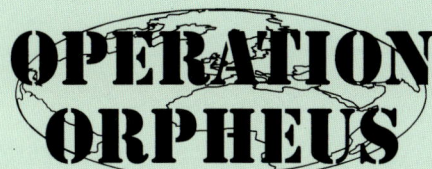

Advice Sheet 2
Survival

1 Never go anywhere alone.

2 If you get into difficulty, blow your whistle.

3 Always carry your first aid kit.

4 Always carry your harness with you.

5 Always carry a torch.

4 When you look at your survival card, you realise that you have already broken two of these rules. Decide which ones these are.

5 Despite Rule Number 1, someone is going to have to go on their own to get help. On your map mark the position of the accident. Decide who is going to get help. Should one person stay with the injured group member or not?

6 You only have one torch between you and its battery is fading fast. You need to memorise the route from the scene of the accident back to Base Camp. Agree a set of directions between you.

7 Continue the scene from here, deciding whether your injured friend lives or dies and what the reaction of the Professor and Pat Adler is to the emergency.

Operation Orpheus 3

Fears Underground

Day 30 A.M.

Since the accident, everyone has been very worried and anxious.

In particular, one group has been having terrible nightmares about strange monsters. There are also rumours about the huge underground lake not far away.

Last night one person was absolutely convinced s/he heard noises during the night. This is what s/he said to you this morning.

It was terrible. I kept waking up and hearing people talking. At least, I think they were people. Then I fell asleep again and had the same dream over and over again. In it I heard echoing whispers. They seemed to follow me right into my sleeping bag. I could see the rocks growing arms and legs, ready to grab me and bury me.

There were worms crawling, slithering towards me, twisting their long bodies around mine, squeezing and crushing me. I could hardly breathe at all.

1 In your groups, talk about the nightmares that you used to have when you lived on the surface and the things that frighten you most.

Operation Orpheus 3

Signs of Life

Day 31

The Professor is so concerned by the effect that the fears and rumours are having on the whole party that it is decided to organise watches throughout the night to try to reassure everyone.

You are on watch with your partner when you hear something suspiciously like a person shouting in the distance. You decide to investigate. In a tunnel 50 metres away from Base Camp you find a message!!

What happens next? Continue this as a play or as a story.

Reflection

In this Unit you have been practising how to

- read to find out information
- answer questions
- write a poem which rhymes
- design and write a pamphlet
- take part in a presentation
- give clear directions
- give a clear account of an experience

Talk to your friends and your teacher about the things you have been doing in this Unit. Decide how much you have understood and how much progress you have made. Filling in Unit 9 of the Record Sheet on page 126 will also help you think about what you have done in this Unit and the knowledge you are gaining in your English lessons.

Record Sheet for Units 7, 8 and 9

Important: Your teacher will give you photocopied versions of these two pages so that you do not need to write in this book.

First of all, with a friend, talk about and decide what the short statements mean. Discuss what you have been practising in English and how much you have understood of what you have done.

Next to each statement there are three targets to aim for. This is what they mean:

I understand this and have practised it.

I have done this with help.

I feel able to do this again.

If you are not sure what a statement means or whether you can do what it says, discuss it with your teacher.

Put a tick under the target that you think best describes what you can do. If you are in doubt, please ask for help.

	Name of Student
	I can
Unit 7	listen with concentration
	justify my opinions in a group
	read and perform a play
	set out speech in a play
	use the exclamation mark
	write a simple message
Unit 8	talk about characters in a story
	put across information and ideas effectively
	express a point of view about a story
	show understanding of how a writer's choice of words affects the reader
	revise and re-draft writing in the light of discussion
	set out speech in a story
	plan and write a complete short story
	keep a diary
	take decisions in a group
Unit 9	read to find out information
	answer questions
	write a poem which rhymes
	design and write a pamphlet
	take part in a presentation
	give clear directions
	give a clear account of an experience

Record of Achievement in English

			Other Comments

Thinking Back

- Which is the best piece of work that you have done so far? Why do you think it was particularly successful?
- Which of the activities in the last three Units did you enjoy most?
- What have you found out about English that you did not know before?
- Was there anything you did not understand and would like more help with?

Thinking Forward

- Where do you think you need to improve most? What can you do to help you do so?
- What kind of activities can you suggest to your teacher that you could do as extra work?

Acknowledgements

cover of *The Demon Headmaster* by Gillian Cross, illustration copyright © Jon Riley 1983, reproduced by permission of Penguin Books Ltd.

extract from *Mindbenders* by Nicholas Fisk, copyright © Nicholas Fisk 1987, reproduced by permission of Penguin Books Ltd.

extract from *Just As Long As We're Together* by Judy Blume, reproduced by permission of William Heinemann Ltd.

extract from *Agent Arthur's Jungle Journey* reproduced by permission of Usborne Publishing Ltd., London

extract from *The Thing in the Woods* by Vivien Alcock, copyright © Vivien Alcock 1989, Hamish Hamilton Children's Books 1989

extract from *Up and Up* by Shirley Hughes, reproduced by permission of The Bodley Head

Mum Dad and Me by James Berry, copyright © 1988 by James Berry, Hamish Hamilton Children's Books 1988

extract from *Mysteries* by Tim Healey, copyright Macdonald Educational 1978, reproduced by permission of Simon and Schuster Young Books, Hemel Hempstead, UK

extract from *The Eighteenth Emergency* by Betsy Byars, reproduced by permission of The Bodley Head

extract from *The Outsiders* by S. E. Hinton reproduced by permission of Victor Gollancz Ltd.

extract from *Animals at Night* by Christopher Tunney, copyright © Grisewood and Dempsey Ltd., 1978, 1987, reprinted by permission of Grisewood and Dempsey Ltd.

extract from *Becky and the Wheels-and-Brake Boys* from *A Thief in the Village and Other Stories* by James Berry (Hamish Hamilton Children's Books 1987), copyright © James Berry 1987

Global Warming material copyright © Friends of the Earth reproduced by kind permission

Poisoned Talk by Raymond Wilson copyright © Raymond Wilson, reproduced by permission of the author

Photographs
Anne Bolt 9
Bruce Coleman Ltd. (Hans Reinhard) 8
Bruce Coleman Ltd. (M. P. L. Fogden) 8
Chris Howes 19, 22
J. Allan Cash Ltd. 19
Chris Ridgers

Thanks also to the staff and pupils of The Dorothy Stringer Secondary School, Preston Park, Brighton, to Longford School and Apple Theatre.

Every effort has been made to trace the copyright holders of the extracts reprinted in this book. The publishers apologise for any inadvertent omissions, which can be rectified in a subsequent reprint.